Developing Students of Influence

Andy Stanley and Stuart Hall

HOWARD BOOKS
A DIVISION OF SIMON & SCHUSTER
New York   London   Toronto   Sydney

To the countless teenagers
around the world who,
in the midst of maximum dynamic pressure,
are allowing their lives to echo loudly in eternity!

Our purpose at Howard Books is to:

- *Increase faith* in the hearts of growing Christians
- *Inspire holiness* in the lives of believers
- *Instill hope* in the hearts of struggling people everywhere

Because He's coming again!

HOWARD
BOOKS

Published by Howard Books, a division of Simon & Schuster, Inc.
1230 Avenue of the Americas, New York, NY 10020
www.howardpublishing.com

Max Q for Youth Leaders © 2004 by Andy Stanley and Stuart Hall

10 Digit ISBN: 1-58229-360-0; 13 Digit ISBN: 978-1-58229-360-8

12 11 10 9 8 7 6 5 4 3

HOWARD colophon is a registered trademark of Simon & Schuster, Inc.

Manufactured in the United States of America

For information regarding special discounts for bulk purchases, please contact: Simon & Schuster Special Sales at 1-800-456-6798 or business@simonandschuster.com.

Edited by Michele Buckingham
Interior design by Stephanie Denney Walker
Cover design by LinDee Loveland and Stephanie Denney Walker

Some of the names used in the stories in this book are not the actual names; identifying details have been changed to protect anonymity. Any resemblance is purely coincidental.

Scripture quotations not otherwise marked are from the *Holy Bible, New International Version®*. Copyright © 1973, 1978, 1984 by International Bible Society. Used by permission of Zondervan. All rights reserved. Scripture quotations marked NLT are taken from the *Holy Bible, New Living Translation*, copyright © 1996. Used by permission of Tyndale House Publishers, Inc., Wheaton, Illinois 60189. All rights reserved. Scripture quotations marked NKJV are taken from the *New King James Version*. Copyright © 1982 by Thomas Nelson, Inc. Used by permission. All rights reserved. Scripture quotations marked *The Message Remix* are taken from *The Message*. Copyright © 1993, 1994, 1995, 1996, 2000, 2001, 2002. Used by permission of NavPress Publishing Group. Scriptures marked NASB are taken from the *New American Standard Bible®*, Copyright © 1960, 1962, 1963, 1968, 1971, 1972, 1973, 1975, 1977, 1995 by The Lockman Foundation. Used by permission.

Contents

Contents

Acknowledgments

Behind every good man is an even better woman;

and behind any project like this one,

there is a host of even greater teammates.

Our deepest thanks and love to:

Our families

for never-ending love, encouragement,

and PlayStation® breaks;

Diane Grant, Dawn Hurley, and Vicki Noblitt

for allowing us to work from our sweet spot;

Dave King and NASA

for your kindness, generosity, and knowledge;

Kevin and Gina Ragsdale

for being uniquely you;

Reggie Joiner and Lanny Donoho

for brains and hearts bigger than most;

the Temple, Scroggins, Walker, Crain,

Joiner, Donoho, Mitchell, and Bowen families

for great counsel and even greater examples;

John Howard and Howard Publishing Company

for believing that teenagers can be influential

without being influenced;

Denny Boultinghouse

for being a friend.

Foreword

When I read this book, I thought to myself, *This is the second Andy Stanley and Stuart Hall book I wish I'd written!* Much like their previous book, *The Seven Checkpoints*, this book breaks new ground for those of us working with students. I loved every chapter! I not only thought about the youth group I pastor, I also thought about my own high-school daughter and how I might help her be the person God wants her to be and help her see her friendships through more influential eyes.

I've been working as a youth pastor for more than twenty-five years, and I know there are limits on what I can do as an individual and on what our youth ministry program can offer. I try to focus on the possible and have faith in God to do the impossible. Andy and Stuart gave me a lot of ideas for the "possible" part of my job as a youth worker.

This book convicted, challenged, and coached me to think more strategically with the core students in my ministry. I don't mean to sound arrogant, but I didn't think that could happen. You see, I'm a champion of teenagers. I've committed my years to helping them and pointing them toward Jesus. I believe in teenagers and have spent the majority of my life believing they can make a difference in this world. Obviously, I'm not alone. I resonated with Andy and Stuart's challenge to help create students of influence—and you will too.

There is a tension in youth ministry we must always battle. The tension involves discipling Christian students and challenging them to care about their lost friends. Both discipleship and evangelism are difficult tasks, and most youth ministries are strong in just one—discipleship. Most youth groups do a good job of providing a safe place for students to grow in Christ—a place where they can be known, loved, and cared for. This is great! But growing in Christ also means developing a passion for the world; it means not only surviving in the world without losing faith but influencing the world because of our faith. A healthy youth ministry is more than simply entertaining Christian kids and keeping them safe from the world.

Max Q challenges youth ministries to be more than just a safe place for kids. It seeks to show how we can develop students to be influential in the world rather than being influenced by the world. I found myself saying, "Yes, I know my kids can do that!" Why should the secular school system challenge teenagers with higher standards than the church does? It's amazing how low the church keeps its expectations of students, while schools raise the bar and say: "If you want to play this sport, give us your summer." "If you want to sing in this choir, you must raise this amount of money." "If you want to be in student leadership, you must attend this camp." And what do kids do? They rise to the levels set before them. What do many youth groups do? They lower the bar and beg students to participate. We under-challenge them!

As I have done in my youth-ministry books and my training seminars, I once again ask you (as a youth worker) to raise your standards for teenagers. Grab a few students whom you believe in. Look them in the eyes and let them know there's a God who is crazy about them and an adult who believes in them. Then cast a vision of who they can become and what they can do when they allow the life-altering Spirit of God to invade their lives, change their character, and give them new eyes for their world.

I challenge you to grab a pad of paper, read this book, ask God for his wisdom, and join Andy and Stuart for a ride that will challenge you, your ministry, and the students that God has entrusted to your care and leadership. Don't let them down . . . raise the bar.

Your friend in youth ministry,

Doug Fields
Youth Pastor, Saddleback Church
Author, *Purpose Driven Youth Ministry*
President; www.simplyyouthministry.com

Christ is the strongest, grandest,
most attractive personality
ever to grace the earth.
But a careless messenger with
the wrong approach can reduce
all this magnificence to
the level of boredom.

JIM RAYBURN

Introduction

I am humbled and amazed at the ministry opportunities God has allowed me to participate in over the past twenty years. And as grateful as I am for the publicity I have received as an author, preacher, and church planter, I have a suspicion that my most fruitful years were actually the years I spent in student ministry. My wife, Sandra, agrees. Every time we see or hear about one of "our" kids doing great things for God, we can't look at each other without tearing up. No words are necessary. We know in our hearts that our time as youth leaders was well spent and that our labors will continue to pay dividends long after we are gone.

Although my student-ministry days have come to an end,

my interest in students and student ministry has not. In fact, it was my concern about what we in the church teach our teenagers that drove me to find a publisher for *The Seven Checkpoints: Seven Principles Every Teenager Needs to Know*, a book that I co-wrote with my friend and colleague Stuart Hall. Stuart is one of the featured communicators at Inside Out, our high-school discipleship environment at North Point Community Church, where I am the senior pastor. He is also the founder of DASH Incorporated, a nonprofit organization that provides resources to help youth leaders develop students of influence.

Two publishers turned the project down. They wanted a book that would have broader distribution. Stuart and I wanted to create a tool for the men and women who have committed a season of their lives to students. I am so grateful to the people at Howard Publishing for getting behind that first project.

The success of *The Seven Checkpoints* and its companion student journal spurred me on to create a second tool for student ministers. *Max Q*, again co-written with Stuart Hall, presents a strategy for equipping students to become influencers in their world. It's designed to help you train Christian teenagers to engage in meaningful relationships with their unchurched, unbelieving friends—while maintaining God-honoring standards, accountability, and a vibrant faith.

As a teenager I grew up in a youth group that discouraged us from having meaningful relationships with non-Christian peers. We were warned to stay away from kids who didn't share our value system. Yet every summer our youth leaders loaded us up and took us on mission trips to other states or countries where we were expected to share the plan of salvation with strangers who apparently didn't embrace our values either. Back home in high school, we were always on the defense, trying not to let the world score on us. But for two hot summer weeks, we were expected to go on the offense in environments where we had absolutely no relational traction.

When I had the opportunity to design a student ministry from the ground up, that inconsistency was the first thing I addressed. I cancelled the annual mission trip and started training kids to be the influence-*ers* rather than the influence-*ees* in their schools and communities. Our youth ministry partnered with them in the evangelism process by creating safe environments where they could bring their unchurched friends. Those early experiments in creating relevant environments formed the basis for much of what we do at North Point Community Church today.

The results were staggering. Every Monday night we had between fifty and sixty students visiting in the homes of friends who had attended one of our invest-and-invite events. Hundreds of kids packed out our midweek outreach events. And hundreds of our core kids saw their friends make professions of faith in Christ.

Much of the content for *Max Q* is taken from a series I repeated almost every year for our students, called "How to Be an Influence without Being Influenced." As you are about to discover, the crux of the series centered on timeless principles that, properly applied, have the potential to equip even the meekest student to become an uncompromising influencer. Adding to that material, Stuart Hall weighs in with insights and illustrations gained from his own ministry to students and leaders around the nation. The result is a tool that we believe will encourage and equip youth leaders and train Christian teenagers to maximize their influence right where they are.

Please understand: This book, like *The Seven Checkpoints*, has very little to do, if anything, with programs. It's not a new evangelism formula. The "rabbit" of youth evangelism and outreach runs far, fast, and wide, and it has been chased long enough. We are convinced that the real problem of lost teenage America is not a lack of evangelism but a lack of substance in the Christian students who live, study, and play among them. The principles we shared in *The Seven Checkpoints* are meant to serve as building blocks for Christian teenagers who desire to become people of substance and influence in their world.

Max Q, too, is a book about substance, and it's about content, not context. We begin to develop students of influence only as we choose to put our focus on the character of our students rather than the charisma of our environments. The breadth and power of our students' influence on their unbelieving friends are directly proportional to the depth of the content of their character. And the effectiveness of our ministries in influencing the unbelieving student culture is absolutely dependent upon the character of our core students.

This book is designed to challenge you, as a youth minister, to redefine what it means to develop spiritually influential students—and provide you with the tools to begin that process. In the pages to come, we will explore what a youth ministry that breeds influence looks like, both in content and context. We will attempt to unravel and understand influence as a principle. We will examine the life of Christ to see

4

how he modeled relational influence.

Each chapter in this book concludes with interactive application questions designed to help you examine and digest what you have read.

To help you further, we have written a companion book, *The Max Q Student Journal*. Similar to the workbook that accompanied *The Seven Checkpoints*, this journal is written for use by your students over a period of several weeks. It is designed to systematically challenge them to understand and apply the six principles of influence we examine in *Max Q*.

The Setup

Two overarching concepts are critical as we develop teenagers of character who are influential in the lives of their peers. We have divided this book into two sections to reflect and organize these concepts: *influence* and *principles*.

The idea of influence is introduced in part 1 and carried throughout part 2. Christian students feel the tension that exists between our desire for them to have healthy friendships and God's call to influence their peers for Christ. We must give them permission to reach out to their lost friends. Part 1 also looks at Jesus, the Master Influencer, and examines the guiding principles of his life, particularly as they relate to influence. We will also examine how the gospel and the sociology of influence must be intertwined to effectively equip our students to be influencers among their peers. Certain common characteristics drive the way all people think and act. Our students need to recognize and understand these characteristics in order to capitalize on their opportunities to be influencers.

The second part of this book focuses on the six key principles that our students must understand and embrace for the sake of becoming influential. We don't believe they're the only principles that are important, but we do believe they are key to the growth of our students. Our students need to learn them first and foremost. We have tried to communicate these six principles of influence in a way that allows them to be easily remembered, understood, and applied. They look like this:

1. The Standards Principle

Our students must develop, be able to verbally articulate, and live by standards.

Standards protect a student's freedom. Standards protect a student's testimony. And standards are the primary tool God will use to open the door for a student to share Christ with a friend. Standards will create the why factor in the life of an unbelieving teenager. Our students must understand how to develop standards and live by them.

2. The Priorities Principle

Our students must prioritize their own spiritual health over the spiritual health of the friends they are attempting to influence.

A time will come when our students will find themselves being drawn into activities they have no business doing. They will find their motivation shifting from influence to acceptance or even romance. When that happens, our students will need to make their own spiritual growth a priority over the spiritual growth of their lost peers. They must recognize when it is time to back off or even bail out. Then they must have the courage to follow through.

3. The Accountability Principle

Our students must maintain effective accountability relationships with other Christian students.

A student's relationship with God is personal—but it is not private. Students who refuse to make themselves accountable to others when it comes to their personal spiritual lives are at greater risk of committing spiritual adultery, just as a man who keeps his personal affairs private is at greater risk of committing adultery against his wife. God never intended for our students to go through life alone.

4. The Unconditional-Acceptance Principle

Our students must love and accept their lost friends unconditionally.

Acceptance is perhaps the strongest desire a teenager possesses. Students will gravitate to people or environments where they sense acceptance and avoid people or environments where they sense rejection. Our students must out-love and out-accept everyone else in an unbelieving peer's life to gain influence.

5. The Sustained-Influence Principle

Our students must sustain influence with their unbelieving peers.

Gaining influence is not enough. Maintaining and sustaining that influence are equally important in the faith journeys

7

of both our core students and their unbelieving friends. Our students must learn how to maintain and sustain their influence once they've gained it.

6. The Leverage Principle

Our students must properly appropriate leverage.

It is always right to share the truth. But to be most effective, our students need to know the best time, place, and method for sharing that truth. They must develop the wisdom to balance the leading of the Holy Spirit, the science of persuasion, and the power of leverage for the sake of influence.

We're convinced that these six principles, if fully engaged, will transform your students and your ministry as they have ours. If these principles are ignored, however, we can almost guarantee that your students will have little to no real influence with their unbelieving peers.

Portrait of an Influential Student

How do we get started? By asking ourselves these questions: What type of students do we want to produce? What do we want our students to look like spiritually, emotionally, and mentally when they graduate? Identifying the characteristics we want our students to have upon graduation is half the battle. As the saying goes, if you don't have a goal, you will hit it every time.

Just as dangerous as having no goal, however, is having a goal or measurement that does not reflect the heart of God. Let's be honest. If our goal in ministry is to produce students with high morals who stay safe, never fail, and never mess up, then we will align our ministries to produce that type of teenager. But if our goal is to develop students of influence, then the components of our ministries must be geared toward helping them along in the process of becoming influential.

It's critical that we as youth ministers keep the end goal foremost in our minds. By clarifying what we want our students to look like when they graduate from our ministries, we make it possible to determine the best process for getting them there. By determining the process, we gain the ability to establish where individual students are in that process. And by establishing where students are in the process, we can then identify the next steps they should take.

Every student within the scope of our influence is at some specific point in the process of becoming spiritually influential. The extremes are wide—from the student who is trying to figure out if God is real, all the way to the teenager who is convinced that his or her life will be best used in full-time vocational ministry. If we have a clear view of our desired end result, it doesn't matter where a student falls on the continuum; the next steps are easy to identify.

So, how does a spiritually influential student compare to the kinds of students we have historically produced from our youth ministries?

Allow us to answer you this way:

Imagine students who can influence their lost peers without being influenced.

Imagine students who are motivated to personally develop rock-solid convictions and unchangeable standards, thus ensuring their spiritual health and continued spiritual growth as they graduate into the great unknown.

Imagine students who take accountability so seriously that they refuse to let each other fall, even as they encourage one another to sustain influence with their lost peers.

Imagine students who so reflect the character of Jesus that they regularly experience the joy of drawing their lost friends to Christ.

Imagine students who actually fulfill their God-given calling to make disciples.

Is this a portrait of the students in your ministry? If not, it can be. And we want to help.

About the Title

Before we dive in, we want to answer another question that's probably running through your mind: What's with the title?

Is Max Q a new superhero? A Disney movie? A maximum-strength cotton swab? And what does it have to do with developing students of influence?

Actually, Max Q is a term used in the space-shuttle program at Kennedy Space Center in Cape Canaveral, Florida. You see, roughly one minute after launch, a space shuttle must withstand a condition of extreme force called "maximum dynamic pressure"—"Max Q" for short. This is the most critical point in flight from an aerodynamics perspective. It's when the most stress is placed on the vehicle. It happens just after the shuttle goes supersonic, at an altitude of 25,000 to 35,000 feet (five to seven miles up).

Dave King, former director of shuttle processing at KSC,

sent us the following perspective from an astronaut friend of his: "I remember seeing equivalent airspeeds of around 455 knots. It's very noticeable to the crew because of something they don't model in the simulator: the wind noise. It's a whistling sound of the wind by the windows, I guess. It gets higher in volume and pitch as we approach Max Q, then the reverse happens as we get beyond it."

According to King, "This is where you hope you did all your homework on the vehicle structure." Mission success demands that all systems on the space shuttle perform at the highest level. When designed properly, prepared carefully, and executed perfectly, the shuttle and its crew safely reach orbital velocity of 17,600 miles per hour at about eight-and-a-half minutes after launch.

We can think of no better illustration to describe what our students experience in their day-to-day lives. They're in a constant state of maximum dynamic pressure. Theirs is a world that moves at a pace of incredible proportion. The "whistling sound of the wind" grows in volume each day. As their youth leaders, we may not hear the volume rising or feel the pressure, but mark it down: They hear it and feel it.

Our role is difficult, yet so significant. We must create a ministry environment that develops students who can withstand intense pressure. Students who can be light in dark places. Students who will not waver from their faith while they passionately pursue relationships with their lost peers. Students who know how to gain influence and earn the privilege to lead.

We serve as launch directors for teenagers who must learn not only to survive but to thrive in Max Q. And that requires the same commitment to excellence that NASA engineers must apply each time they launch a space shuttle. Anything less is a recipe for disaster.

The countdown has already started.

Will your students be ready for liftoff?

PART ONE

The Truth about Influence

The great reformer Martin Luther once said,

> If I profess with the loudest voice and clearest exposition every portion of the Truth of God except precisely that point which the world and the devil are at that moment attacking, I am not confessing Christ. Where the battle rages, there the loyalty of the soldier is proved. And to be steady on all the battlefield is merely flight and disgrace if he flinches at that point.

As youth leaders we can spend all of our time, energy, and resources developing and maintaining the greatest programs, the coolest environments, and the best-behaved students within the four walls of the church. But that's not the battlefront. The point of attack comes elsewhere. The battle takes place at precisely that point where teenagers who know Jesus personally must invest in lost friends and influence peers who desperately need Christ.

Too many youth ministries flinch at this point. May we flinch no more.

Let people feel
the weight of who you are
and let them deal with it.

JOHN ELDREDGE

Granting Permission

Creating a Ministry of Influence

It was Saturday morning, February 1, 2003. In perhaps the greatest tragedy in space exploration history, seven courageous heroes lost their lives that day. The space shuttle Columbia, returning from a sixteen-day mission to outer space, reentered the earth's atmosphere at more than eighteen times the speed of sound and, only minutes from its scheduled landing, disintegrated some 207,000 feet over Texas. Most of us will never forget where we were on that fateful morning. Our hearts broke and mourned with the families of those seven astronauts, many of whom were gathered on a runway at Kennedy Space Center in Florida awaiting their loved ones' safe return. Columbia and her crew were lost only sixteen minutes from home.

It will most likely take the sharpest and brightest minds years to determine the specific cause of this horrific loss. We may never know the full extent of the truth. But one thing is certain: Columbia, in the midst of experiencing maximum dynamic pressure, when she needed to be the strongest, was weak. Perhaps her weakness was minute; perhaps it was greater than we'll ever know. Regardless of the degree, the fact remains that at the moment of the most intense heat and pressure, Columbia's integrity was compromised. And what was to be a defining, triumphant moment became a terribly destructive one.

The State of Max Q

Somewhere at that edge where earth's atmosphere ends and the greater reaches of outer space begin exists a point of tension and stress so extreme and intense that it cannot be simulated. It is a state known by people much smarter than most of us as "maximum dynamic pressure," or "Max Q" for short. Any object intent on leaving the earth's atmosphere must pass through it. Nothing and no one can evade it. It cannot be ignored. For a space shuttle to pass successfully through Max Q, every system must be executing perfectly; every person must be operating at the highest level of training and alertness; and the integrity of the spacecraft must be strong and fully functional.

It's not much of a stretch to parallel the state of Max Q as it relates to space exploration to the pressures our Christian students face as they strive to become young men and women of influence in their world. In fact, the comparisons are hauntingly similar.

Youth-ministry leaders get to observe up close the

intense pressure that society exerts on teenagers today. We understand—at least in theory—that in order to withstand the pressure without being influenced by it, our students must live at a very high level of wisdom, purity, and courage. But how many of our students are actually being trained to operate at that level?

Sadly, not many. According to statistics, over three-fourths of Christian teenagers, after graduating from high school, will abandon the church—and possibly even their faith.[1]

For years we have watched as Christian homes and youth ministries have sent graduates headlong into Max Q. Too often the results have been as tragic as the loss of the space shuttle. Reeling under the intense pressure, many students get suckered into making poor choices. Or they become magnetized to lifestyles that don't match their stated belief system.

The culture in which our students live has cornered the market on generating maximum dynamic pressure. Popular music, for example, is an exercise of attitudes and word imageries that promote immorality, sexual promiscuity, violence, and disrespect. The accompanying videos merely "color in" the outlines the songs have already made in the minds of their young listeners. Meanwhile, magazines and other media add pressure by promoting a standard of physical beauty that few human beings can attain. As a result, an increasing number of teenagers are developing eating disorders. More and more students are pursuing breast implants, liposuction, and other forms of plastic surgery. They're convinced they must have abs of steel and match Hollywood's latest hottie from head to toe in looks and physical appeal.

What were considered pressures reserved for college life—drugs, alcohol, sex—have now trickled down to the high-school, junior-high, and even elementary-school campus. The drug of choice may fluctuate from marijuana to cocaine to ecstasy, but it's readily available. So is alcohol. There is an unspoken implication here: Not only are teenagers engaging in harmful behavior, they are rebelling against authority and disobeying the law. They are not establishing moral boundaries. For large numbers of them, the end of innocence is coming sooner, rather than later.

Perhaps the most intense point of Max Q for students lies in the arena of friends. Acceptance is, of course, one of the strongest needs teenagers have. Most of our students will never admit it; but fitting in, being accepted, and having a sense of belonging with a person or group is their highest priority. (Let's be honest: It's a priority for all of us.) As youth leaders and workers, we have all witnessed the lengths teenagers will go to gain this elusive and fleeting acceptance from their peers. Most of us remember how powerful that desire was for us when we were their age.

Society, culture, peer pressure—these, along with numerous other obvious and not-so-obvious dynamics, combine to create a state of maximum dynamic pressure. It's invisible, but our students feel it. Our students are affected by it. And ultimately, our students have to deal with it.

Or do they?

The Paradox

Some Christian parents and youth ministers would argue that it's their job and duty to protect their teenagers from the influence and pressures of the world. We would all agree that it's not healthy for our students to have close relationships with peers who are foolish, rebellious, and not believers. As we stated in our previous book, *The Seven Checkpoints*, friendships have a big influence on the quality and direction of a teenager's life. In fact, friends can be more influential than parents, youth leaders, faith—even God.

For a student to connect with someone in friendship who does not hold the same values, believe in the same God, and desire the same lifestyle can be very destructive. And precisely because the potential for negative consequences is so great, we as parents and youth leaders tend to build strong, inflexible "friendship boundaries" around our teens. For many solid Christian students, bringing a new friend home to meet the parents is the equivalent of trying to get through airport security with a pocket full of change and a pistol in your bag. Why is there such scrutiny? Because we know how harmful a wrong choice of friends can be.

So we encourage—if not exactly force—our students to acquire and maintain friendships only from within the pool of Christian teenagers at church and youth group. And what happens? Subtly over time these students begin to grow more and more distant from their culture and from their peers who need Christ. Our youth ministries turn into shelters from the storm. Most of our evangelism efforts become frustrating and futile attempts on the part of our core students to bridge the ever-widening gap between themselves and their lost peers— in hopes of getting at least one new person to an event at church so the youth pastor will get off their backs.

We're giving our students a conflicting message. We know that Christians are called by Jesus to "go and make disciples" (Matthew 28:19). So we tell our students to reach out to their unbelieving peers—even as we plead with them to keep their friendships within Christian circles. We trap our core students within a fluctuating ping-pong game of "Go! No! Go! No!"

It doesn't help that our concept of "going and making disciples" is often centered more on modern student-evangelism strategies than on biblical disciple making. We put a hyper-focus on "going" and take a drudgery-type approach to "making disciples." This may sound blasphemous, but "making disciples" is not accomplished most effectively through door-to-door witnessing, mall blitzes, or sharing the Four Spiritual Laws. And it's not accomplished most effectively through our typical Christian education models and strategies.

Disciplism

No, the most effective way to carry out the Great Commission—the way to "go and make disciples" as God intends, even in the midst of Max Q—is to marry the concepts of evangelism and discipleship as we've known them. We've coined the word *disciplism* ("disciple," with an "ism") to best describe this union of ideas, strategies, and obedience to God's Word. Disciplism means more than witnessing to someone. It means investing your life into the lives of your unbelieving friends. It means purposefully engaging the culture and your friends in the culture in order to influence them with the gospel. Once you've influenced them, it means walking alongside them as they grow in their faith.

Disciplism is not a call you can answer via satellite. It's a hands-on, on-location challenge. And it's the very heart of God—his reason for coming to earth in the form of a man: to proclaim his glory by serving and dying for all.

There is a reason why so many of us in youth ministry seem to avoid God's idea of disciple making. It is a deeply theological concept: Making disciples—disciplism—is *hard*. For students to invest their lives into the lives of their peers takes energy, time, and sometimes money. It often takes blood, sweat, and tears. Making disciples means that their priorities have to change. Their schedules have to change. Their lifestyles have to change. And the implementation of disciplism means that *our* philosophies and ideologies as youth leaders have to change too.

To Err Is Trouble

The potential exists for us to err on one of two extremes—and either extreme is dangerous. On the one hand, if our students have the healthiest of Christian friendships, yet never influence their unbelieving friends for the sake of Christ, have we been successful? Is goodness our standard in youth ministry, or godliness? Behavior modification is not our goal: Transformation is. It would be a tragedy for us to settle for developing good students rather than students of greatness.

Ask yourself this question: Has my idea of success in youth ministry been to make sure that my students don't "drink, smoke, chew, or date those who do?" Our hearts hurt when we think of the students who were exposed to a deranged idea of social reform rather than spiritual renewal under our leadership. We confess: Behavior modification is a much easier road to travel and one we have regretfully traveled.

On the other hand, if our students immerse themselves in their culture and develop friendships with lost peers but then cave in under the pressure and fall into sin, what have we gained? God doesn't want us to play chess with our students, risking their character and integrity and ignoring the consequences for the sake of his kingdom (and ours). He has not called us to be reckless.

He has, however, called our students to influence their friends. It is the right thing for them to do. And the fact is, most of the time the right thing to do is hard. The right thing to do is full of risk. There are no promises of ease or safety in following Jesus. No guarantees. Just his promise that "I will never leave you or forsake you." That he is with you always. And understanding this leads us to ask some pretty hefty questions: What happens if we don't do what we know is right? What happens if we do?

Several years ago these questions forced us to take a hard look at our ideas of evangelism and discipleship within the context of youth ministry. Reaching students for Christ was and is our driving force. We've always believed God is passionate about teenagers, and we want to be passionate about what burns in God's heart. We want to lead teenagers into a growing relationship with Jesus Christ. And we believe that the greatest influence in a teenager's life was and still is another teenager.

What we found when we "opened the hood" of our ministry, however, was discouraging. Our methodology pointed to a painful truth: We were more consumed with creating evangelistic environments than with developing influential students. Our calendars and our prayers, we realized, were geared primarily towards programs rather than personal development. But the most obvious sign that we were missing the mark came from our own core students, who could not seem to maintain leverage with their lost peers.

These bleak observations caused us to dive deep into the concepts of student evangelism and influence—theologically, practically, and programmatically. We decided to start at square one and reconstruct our philosophy from scratch.

Permission Granted

The beginning of our journey brought us to an interesting word: *permission.*

We're not rocket scientists, but we think the odds are pretty high that your students have at least a few acquaintances who are not Christians. And those students feel a certain tension regarding these friends. Is it okay to get close to them? Will they be judged by God or their Christian friends for reaching out to unbelievers? Should they feel guilty for having lost friends?

Well, let us ask you: Is it God's will for your students to have non-Christian friends?

Apparently the early church battled with this very dilemma. Paul specifically addressed the hyperreaction of the church in Corinth to a challenge he had previously given. His response to their reaction is recorded in 1 Corinthians 5:

> I wrote you in my letter not to associate with immoral people; I did not at all mean with the immoral people of this world, or with the covetous and swindlers, or

23

with idolaters, for then you would have to go out of the world. But actually, I wrote to you not to associate with any so-called brother if he is an immoral person, or covetous, or an idolater, or a reviler, or a drunkard, or a swindler—not even to eat with such a one. (1 Corinthians 5:9–11 NASB)

Even though his earlier letter is not included in the New Testament, Paul implies in verse 9 that he had previously written to the church in Corinth, instructing them not to associate with immoral people. Apparently the Corinthian church misinterpreted this directive. For some reason the Corinthian believers—like so many of us—thought that Paul's message to separate themselves from immoral people meant they were to steer clear of people who did not know God. They assumed he meant they should put as much distance as possible between themselves and the "pagans."

Paul, however, was not referring to the people who didn't know God. And in this passage in 1 Corinthians 5, he cleared up the misunderstanding—for the Corinthians and for us. When he said that believers should not associate with immoral people, he did not mean the immoral people of this world. He was referring to people who claim to be Christians (so-called brothers) who continue in the active practice of sin. Paul says we should not even eat with such a person!

Out of This World

It seems that Paul sensed the absurdity of the response of the Corinthian church when he said that in order to disassociate

24

with immoral people, we would have to "go out of the world." In other words, lost people are all around us. We would have to leave this planet to get away from them. If we as youth ministers don't want our students to associate with their lost peers, we need to move them to Mars.

Now understand: We are both parents. We recognize and take seriously the pressures of the world our children live in. With our wives we have prayed constantly for their purity of heart and mind. We've worked extremely hard to protect them from the negative influences that can creep in so subtly through unhealthy friendships, television, movies, and music.

But we've had to ask ourselves: Isn't our role as parents (and youth leaders) to ground our children in the things of God so they can be influential without being influenced? Won't they have to stand on their own two feet in this world one day anyway?

Isn't the major task of our children's existence on this earth, like our own, to know God and make him known? And if so, doesn't a large part of our leadership in their lives need to center on helping them be able to do this—to exist for the glory of God? To be a part of the redemption of another human soul for the name and fame of God? How can we run from that responsibility? Who is going to reach the world if we're teaching our children and students to run from it?

Here Comes the Judge

Paul completes his comments this way: "For what have I to do with judging outsiders? Do you not judge those who are within the church? But those who are outside, God judges.

REMOVE THE WICKED MAN FROM AMONG YOURSELVES"
(1 Corinthians 5:12–13 NASB).

Paul is very clear that we are to judge those within the church. Better stated, you and I are to hold each other accountable. Our students are to hold each other accountable. But they have no right to judge those unbelieving friends who act and think immorally; God reserves that position for himself. Their lost friends have never chosen to play by God's rules. Here is a major announcement brought to us by the God of the universe: Lost teenagers act lost.

Our students can't stand as judges in the lives of their friends who don't know Christ. What they *can* do is love them and seek to be influential in their lives. And we must give them permission to do so. For too long we as parents and youth leaders have nailed a No Trespassing sign on the entry to this greatest of adventures, disciplism. But that sign does not reflect the heart of God.

Let's be very clear: We are by no means implying that our students should be reckless and put their lives at risk by becoming a "companion of fools" (Proverbs 13:20). It is vital that our students have strong and healthy relationships with Christian friends. In fact, those relationships should be a priority.

But let's also be clear: As believers, our students can't ignore God's challenge to reach out to their unbelieving world. To do so would be as wrong and destructive as ignoring God's wisdom to not walk with fools.

That leaves youth leaders with a daunting, yet urgent, task: We must develop students who can be influential without being influenced. Admittedly, this is a high-wire act that must be walked with balance and precision. But we must teach our students how to embrace the tension—how to live with it without being destroyed by it. We must raise up students who can flourish spiritually and influentially, even while being pressed on every side.

Keep It Simple

Developing students of influence isn't easy, but it's not complicated either. Reggie Joiner, our family-ministries pastor at North Point Community Church, has crafted a statement that best summarizes the core of youth ministry:

> We must build bridges of relationship strong enough to bear the weight of the truth we have to give.

Sadly, the validity and significance of this statement easily gets lost in the giant array of strategies, facilities, conferences, and events that make up what we call youth ministry today. Over time the core essentials—relationships and truth—fade from the priority list. They become like objects in the rearview mirror of a car that's speeding away, barely visible in the dust.

What we need is a major shift toward simplification. We must strip away the complex layers of ministry veneer that we have allowed to build up over time.

One of the most eye-opening parts of our journey toward a ministry focused on developing students of influence was the difference between the perceived and actual time our youth ministry team had to invest in the lives of our students. By factoring in the national average of annual attendance of core students (roughly 70 percent) and subtracting for such variables as sickness, family vacations, and school functions, we determined that in a fifty-two-week year, we had at best thirty-five programmatic times with our teenagers. That is not a lot of time! When we combined this fact with the fact that our students had an awful lot to learn and become in order to develop as influencers, two key elements became very evident: (a) we needed to reduce the content for developing students of influence to several key central themes and principles; and (b) we needed to increase the time our youth leaders had to invest these principles into the lives of students by reducing the time they spend on programs in church.

In other words, we had to do more by doing less.

We cannot simulate the pressure of the world within the four walls of the church. For us to continually fill up our calendars with programs to keep teens out of harm's way, off the streets, and away from Max Q does not negate the fact that they will spend five days a week for several years in junior high and high school, four or more years in college, and the rest of their lifetimes in the work force. These places are the spiritual epicenter of Max Q. For this reason it makes sense to decrease the amount of time we (and our ministry team leaders) spend with students within our four walls and increase the time we spend developing relational leverage with those same students outside our weekly programs. Time is a limited commodity; we must optimize it for its greatest impact.

One very practical way we found to apply the "less is more" principle was to change our weekly outreach environment to a quarterly one. Now, we understand that weekly outreach programs can be good. Often they are effective. One might argue that making a decision to switch from a weekly event to a quarterly event moves us *away* from influence, not toward it. How can four outreaches a year possibly top twenty-six?

But let's think about it. Coming up with creative programs week after week to attract unbelieving teenagers is not easy. On the contrary, it's quite difficult, and that's one of the reasons most weekly environments eventually begin to look and feel the same. The result is that these outreach environments wind up being attended predominantly by Christian students. We slowly but surely end up salting salt.

And there's another problem. As we were starting on this journey, we spoke to many unbelieving teenagers who told us they didn't believe our core Christian students really cared about them personally; they thought our students only cared about getting them to church. Why? Because our students were coming to them every week and inviting them to our outreach environment—and that was their only effort at making contact. Our students, because they were relationally withdrawn from their lost peers, did not have the relational leverage they needed to get their friends to believe they cared, much less accept their repeated invitations.

We know of several youth ministries around the country that, like North Point, have made the difficult decision to reduce their number of purposeful outreach environments from weekly to monthly or quarterly. These ministries tell us they have been able to focus their energies on encouraging their core students to build relational bridges with their lost peers without the pressure of always having to invite them to church events. Now when these ministries plan an outreach event, their students have one to three months to gain relational leverage with their friends, and the leadership team has sufficient time to make sure the programming is powerful, seeker-friendly, creative, fun, thought provoking, and life changing. We continue to hear reports that the results have been extraordinary!

Leadership Is Influence

If you haven't caught on already, there is a constant theme that runs through these thoughts about keeping things simple: leadership. Leadership is not just something that a few of us do because of the titles on our office doors. Leadership is *everything* to effective youth ministry and the process of developing students of influence. Social scientists tell us we can have direct influence on a maximum of eight people. That means that you and I, the moment we were hired, were not suddenly influential in the lives of every person encompassed within our ministries. We simply couldn't be. We can't be. It's impossible. That's why, from the top down, in each of our ministries, the development of leadership must be a priority.

Perhaps leadership development wasn't part of the bill of goods you bought into upon entering the world of youth ministry. Chances are, you are in this simply because you love God and love students. Perhaps the term *leadership*, to your way of thinking, means adult chaperones for your trips, "parent police" for your outreach environments, and a sounding board for your ideas. But scoot up to the edge of your chair, lean in, and read this carefully: Unless we develop a team of adults to be influential and then mobilize them to become developers of influencers themselves, even our best attempts at developing students of influence will fall short.

Simply stated, leadership is influence. For many of us, the lack of leadership development in our ministries is the "bushel" that keeps our students from becoming lights in the darkness and cities on a hill.

It may even be our state of Max Q.

Leading from the Heart of the Matter

Of course, we can't give what we don't have. And we can't lead to places we've never been ourselves.

As youth leaders, we have the rare potential to order our lives in a way that will not only affect the lives of other human beings, but the course of history, as well. The teenagers we influence today will be the world-changers and world-influencers of tomorrow. But let's admit it: Most of us find ourselves at one time or another so focused on teenagers and "the ministry" that we neglect to nurture and examine our own hearts. And when it's dark *inside*, that darkness will eventually manifest itself *outside*. When we neglect the deepest parts of ourselves, that neglect will begin to affect those parts that are most visible.

The best youth leaders work from a place of passion and character within their own hearts. If they don't, they can't inspire, they can't lead, and they can't model the influential life.

It takes courage to lead from the heart. To do so means that we are standing and living for things we believe in—things that burn like a branding iron in our souls. We are professing

31

values that are important to us. But know this: We will always be targets when we lead that way. In fact, go ahead and draw a huge bull's-eye on yourself right now, because desiring to build a ministry that's intent on developing students of influence will draw friendly and unfriendly fire. There will be pastors and parents and students who will not understand what you're doing, and some of them will be pretty good shots.

Leading from the heart definitely brings a degree of tension and pain. But to not lead from the heart, we've found, has consequences that are even more painful. Not leading from the heart results in preaching a divided message. Affirming something inwardly yet behaving in a completely different way outwardly. Living in a constant state of awareness of what we *should be* versus what we *are*, what we *should do* versus what we *are doing*. How excruciating! Unfortunately, many youth ministers feel this pain today. We have written this book because we don't want you to be one of them.

Mark it down: Choosing to build a ministry of influence will lead you into some scary places. You'll learn things about your heart that you haven't had to face before. Quite a few "bogeymen" lurk beneath the shallow ideas of modern student ministry; but to keep them below the surface is the equivalent of giving Sammy Sosa more creatine or cork—they will only grow stronger.

Don't give in to the bogeymen. Instead, dream big!

Dreaming the Impossible Dream

Dream big? We can hear a few hearts balking: "With all the pressure that's already on me from my pastor, my staff, and parents to get students into the building on Sundays or Wednesdays, isn't it OK for me to just program my way to success? Do I really have to dream bigger than that? We've purchased so much expensive equipment, built this new facility, prepared these great games, and it's working . . . sort of. Isn't this the best way for me to reach teenagers, protect my job, and provide for my family?"

Well, small dreams are certainly great if you want to always meet your goals. Job security will almost be a lock.

But small dreams are also great if you never want to move beyond the status quo. Small dreams are great if you desire to produce religious teenagers. Small dreams are great if you think spiritual influence only happens if you're a preacher, a singer, or a missionary. Small dreams are great if you enjoy mediocrity. If you want to produce "good" teenagers, then dream a tiny dream for your students.

There is one big problem with such a small dream: Our God isn't small. And if God isn't small, then his dreams aren't small. In fact, the dreams that God has for each of us—and especially for our teenagers—are definitely not small. God dreams big for our students. If our hearts are going to be in tune with his heart, we must dream big too.

Running the Gauntlet

In many ways, this matter of developing students of influence is like a fork in the road for us. We can either choose to dream big, lead from the heart, simplify our ministries, pour ourselves into others, develop adult leaders and students of real substance, build bridges of relationship and thus create a culture of influence; or we can go the way of so many youth ministries and depend on programs to reach teenagers. Which road will we take?

A movie that has been popular with our two families in recent years is *First Knight,* an account of King Arthur's Camelot from a unique perspective. In one great scene, a huge festival is being held in Camelot. One of the attractions of the festival is a gauntlet—an extreme obstacle course of sharp swinging blades, huge logs and stones, and constantly moving platforms. Men put on the equivalent of a bed mattress and try to walk from one end of the gauntlet to the other without getting knocked off or—worst-case scenario—being decapitated.

The soon-to-be queen promises a kiss to any man who can conquer the gauntlet, a feat that no one has ever accomplished. That's when Lancelot (played by Richard Gere) steps up and, with no padding at all, defeats the gauntlet—thus becoming the first person to do so and winning the prize.

King Arthur (Sean Connery) is amazed at Lancelot's feat of courage, athleticism, and quick thinking, so he strikes up a conversation that would serve us all well to consider. When King Arthur asks Lancelot how he conquered the gauntlet, Lancelot answers, "It is not hard to know where the danger is if you watch it coming."

"Others have tried and failed. You were the first," King Arthur says.

"Perhaps fear made them go back when they should have gone forward," Lancelot responds.[2]

The state of Max Q exists in the student culture as surely as it exists at the edge of the earth's atmosphere. It also exists in youth ministry. Perhaps fear has gripped our hearts for far too long. Instead of going forward, we have taken steps backward. But to exist as God created us to exist, to do ministry as God intended for us to do it, we must face the danger. It isn't hard to know where the danger is when we can see it coming. Our students are ready and able to rise to a new level of expectation. They are ready to become influencers among their peers and in their world.

Are you afraid? Then push forward!

Pressure Points

1. In your opinion what are the top five elements of student culture that create the state of Max Q?

2. Interview at least ten of your core students this week. Try to determine who their best friends are and if they have intentional relationships with unbelieving peers. Record your findings and thoughts.

3. Which do you spend the most time investing in: creating outreach environments or developing students of influence? Why?

4. Read through the Gospels and the book of Acts. How do you think Jesus and the new church developed a culture of influence?

5. What will be the greatest challenges to simplifying your ministry in order to focus on leadership development?

The purpose of the church
cannot be to survive
or even to thrive but to serve.
And sometimes servants
die in the serving.

ERWIN RAPHAEL MCMANUS

2

Knowing What to Expect

Lessons from the Master Influencer

In almost any town in America, searching for a church with some form of youth ministry is like going to the food court at the mall. Not long ago Stuart traveled to a major metropolitan city for a speaking engagement. En route from the airport, he tried to count the number of churches he passed along the main highway. He lost track after thirty-two. There were thirty-two-plus churches on a fifteen- to twenty-mile stretch of road!

The sheer number of church and youth-group options teenagers have today begs a question: What motivates students to bypass church after church and ultimately land at *your* youth group? Why do they pass churches bigger or smaller, richer or poorer, in sickness or in health (it fits), with excellent programming or little excellence at all, to come to yours?

We hesitate to ask for fear that some may wrongly assume that youth leaders and youth ministries are in competition with one another for students. We all know that's not the case, don't we? We're too spiritually mature to compete like that (big wink). We pray we are stating the obvious when we say that our competition is not with each other. But the answer to this question takes us to the very core of why this book exists.

What Teenagers Want

The reasons behind a teenager's magnetic pull toward one church and total disregard for another will vary. Certain reasons will always lie in the realm of mystery. A few, however, are certain.

Safety

Students are looking for an environment where they can feel safe—where they can put away the false pretenses that so many church traditions have tended to erect. Unfortunately, the church, as many of them have known it, (and as we, their leaders, have made it) is not always a place where vulnerability is valued. So when a church or youth ministry comes along that communicates warmth, safety, and spiritual health, students are drawn.

Relevance

Students are also attracted when the simplicity of the gospel is communicated in a relevant way. Most teenagers could care less about reciting by memory the names of all sixty-six books of the Bible. What they want to know is whether or not the message within those sixty-six books relates to them. Their constant question is, "Does this truth relate to me? And if it doesn't, does it relate at all?"

Fun

Just as relevance is a must to this generation, so is fun. We're not suggesting that youth leaders have to continually top the previous week's program in order to show teenagers a good time. Chasing that rabbit down the "funny trail" is exhausting. But the truth is, students are much more willing to apply truth to their lives if they can have fun while they're doing it.

Authenticity

More than any other people group, teenagers have very sensitive "bogus detectors." They want a church or youth group environment that is real—one with substance and authenticity. They also want leaders who live out what they proclaim lives within them. Few things offend a teenager more than a spiritual leader who claims one thing but lives another.

Experience

Students want to be a part of something that reflects what the true church *should* reflect. By "the church" we mean individuals who gather collectively in the name of Jesus with the express purpose of existing for his name and glory—not a building. If God is real, then teenagers want to experience him as he is and not as religious people have made him out to be.

This generation would much rather feed the hungry, build homes for the homeless, and care for the hurting than gather in our enormous facilities and pay homage to ourselves. In fact, it is frightening to think that we have built so many large church facilities that will be inherited by a generation that could care less about them. Today's students don't want to *go* to church. They want to *be* the church.

Finding the Balance

It might be easy to conclude from these insights that the key to developing students and a youth ministry of influence is context. And the truth is, environment is very important. Creating an energetic, dynamic context or environment in which students feel welcomed, engaged, and safe is difficult but necessary. Even the physical environment matters. We have all seen the effects an antiseptic room can have on high school students. Even teens with attention deficit hyperactive disorder and five Surge drinks in their system get depressed in a facility that exudes no imagination or creativity!

However, we would be terribly off balance if we assumed that context is the key to reaching students. Context is important, but it's not the key. Far from it. A quick glance at the variety of highly influential youth ministries across the country attests to this fact. These churches vary in size, programming excellence, and creativity. Budgets vary from peanuts to a whole lot of cheese. Facilities range from sterile portables to ESPN-Zone-type megabuildings.

What is their common denominator? They all have core students who are influential—students who have built strong relational bridges with their peers.

This makes sense. Environment matters. What you and I do matters. But the greatest influence on a teenager is another teenager. Where we as youth leaders tend to rattle out of balance is in choosing to spend so much time, energy, and money on developing our outreach programs and facilities—while neglecting the character and substance of the students who are the most significant magnetic force.

Granted, most of us at some point have taught our students how to share their faith, how to answer tough questions, and how to lead a friend to Christ. We have exhausted every resource in canvassing neighborhoods, throwing pizza blasts, and offering special-emphasis weekends. But are these things equivalent to developing students of influence? What should our ministries—or, more accurately, our *students*—be reflecting to other teenagers? To find this answer, let's look at what the Bible has to say about the early church.

Reflecting Jesus

We'll pick up the story in Acts 8. Saul was standing by, watching Stephen being stoned for his faith. He was even helping out by holding the robes of those who were doing the stoning. Saul hated Christ, Christianity, and, most of all, Christians. His sole purpose in life was to snuff out the movement of Christianity once and for all.

And Saul was there, giving approval to Stephen's death.

On that day a great persecution broke out against the church at Jerusalem, and all except the apostles were scattered throughout Judea and Samaria. Godly men buried Stephen and mourned deeply for him. But Saul began to destroy the church. Going from house to house, he dragged off men and women and put them in prison. (Acts 8:1–3)

Did you see it? Saul was leading the persecution against the church, and notice what that *did not* mean: Saul was not vandalizing facilities or painting graffiti on the walls. He wasn't burning down buildings. He was dragging *people* to prison! Read on:

Meanwhile, Saul was still breathing out murderous threats against the Lord's disciples. He went to the high priest and asked him for letters [arrest warrants] to the synagogues in Damascus, so that if he found any there who belonged to the Way, whether men or women, he might take them as prisoners to Jerusalem. As he neared Damascus on his journey, suddenly a light from heaven flashed around him. He fell to the ground and heard a voice say to him, "Saul, Saul, why do you persecute me?"

"Who are you, Lord?" Saul asked.

"I am Jesus, whom you are persecuting," he replied. (Acts 9:1–6)

Persecuting Jesus? Saul wasn't persecuting Jesus. He was persecuting Jewish Christians. Jesus was already dead, alive again, and gone. Saul never even met Jesus. How could he be persecuting Jesus? Here's how: Jesus was so closely associated with the church that when Saul persecuted people (the church), he was persecuting Jesus!

42

Scripture clearly teaches that the church is an extension and should be a reflection of the person of Jesus Christ. Developing students of influence means that we develop students who reflect the purposes and personality of Jesus.

Let's be honest. To the large majority of unbelieving teenagers, the church has a reflection problem. Lost students are not ticked off at a building. They are not apathetic toward our youth rooms. Most are not even angry with God. No, unbelieving teenagers distance themselves from *Christians*. Our facilities and programs have very little to do with it.

And the Christians who experience that distance the most are our students.

If you don't believe we in the church at large have a reflection problem, ask your core students: Based on what you have seen and heard, how do you think your church would fill in this blank: The Christian life is _____?

Their answers will probably astonish you. Granted, perception is the cruelest form of reality. But the students we interviewed for this book responded across the spectrum— from the extreme of lots of rules and dos and don'ts to the opposite of "whatever makes you feel good," all grace and no truth, and so on. And these were Christian students! Can you imagine what their unbelieving peers think?

Jesus' purpose was very clear. The Gospels are four books written by four different men who walked with, talked with, and observed Jesus and his closest followers. What pours out of these pages of truth is so evident that it's heartbreaking when compared to our distorted reflection. The reason Jesus existed was to seek and save that which was lost. His purpose was to reconnect the disconnected. He existed to bring his Father glory—and the best means to bring God glory was to bridge the gap between sinful man and holy God, which he did through his redemptive death on the cross.

We all must connect to God through Christ. That means our primary task as youth leaders is to connect teenagers to God through the person of Jesus Christ. And how do we connect teenagers to Jesus? Through the church. The church is not a building, a context, or a meeting. It is the uniquely individual people who have placed their faith and trust in Christ.

Our students are the church. They're not the church of tomorrow; they're the church of now. And when their hearts begin to connect to the personality and purposes of Christ, the embryonic stages of influence begin.

What Jesus Looked Like

Of course, we all have our biased pictures of what we think Jesus looked like and acted like. Perhaps we think of Ralph Kozak's well-known rendering, "Jesus Laughing." Or maybe we think of that picture many of us saw in childhood of Jesus holding a lamb across his shoulders. But a detailed reading of the gospel accounts makes clear that Jesus is not the meek and mild individual so many of us have thought him to be. His personality can be summed up best in four characteristics:

1. Authentic

For Jesus, authenticity was of paramount importance. He had zero patience for the traditions of man. He was all about the real truth—and that set him in a constant battle. Just as

Spiderman has the Green Goblin, Batman has the Joker, and Luke has Darth Vader, Jesus had the Pharisees. They were his archenemies. Why? Because they were pretentious, pious, and unauthentic religious leaders. Jesus so valued authenticity that he confronted those people who were considered the most religious with their lack of realness.

How does this relate to our students? Unfortunately, to many unbelieving teenagers, our Christian students seem as pretentious, pious, and unauthentic as the Pharisees and Michael Jackson's nose. Part of this is because of the "separation of church and state," if you will. Our students tend to so remove themselves from any relationships or dealings with their lost peers that those peers begin to view them as "holier than thou." What an unbelieving teenage culture needs to see are students who are loving Christ passionately and who are also loving life—not just enduring life.

Being authentic means that our students are in touch with the heartbeat of their peers. It means they are not afraid to show that they hurt, fear, and care. It may mean they admit they don't have all the answers. It definitely means they refuse to hide behind Sunday-school clichés and choose, instead, to live in the real world with a real God who is real life!

2. Relevant

Even though Jesus was from a different realm, he was always relevant to his culture. Reggie Joiner defines being *relevant* as "using what is cultural to communicate what is timeless."[1] Whether relating a biblical concept to sowing, reaping, fishing, a widow's coin, a lost sheep, or a host of other practical illustrations, Jesus used what people were familiar with to engage their hearts and minds and communicate truths with both eternal implications and practical applications.

There were plenty of prophets and teachers during the time Jesus walked the earth. What separated Christ from these teachers—apart from the fact that he was God—was that when Jesus spoke, people not only listened; they retained what they heard. People were always amazed at his teachings because they seemed to have a power that others lacked. Jesus taught with "takeaway" power: People took away something when he taught.

Our students must develop the personality of Christ by using what is cultural to communicate what is timeless. Their peers want to know how truth relates to them in their world. They want to see the God-life lived out in the here and now and not just spoken of in the sweet by and by.

3. Enjoyable

One thing the Gospels make clear: Jesus was always the life of the party. People wanted to be near him. Even children and sinners felt welcome around him. Without a doubt, hanging around Jesus was an enjoyable experience!

Our students should be the kind of people their lost peers enjoy being around. It should be fun to hang out with them. And our ministry environments should be an experience that teenagers can't wait to get to and don't want to miss!

If joy is missing from a believer's personality DNA, isn't there a problem? If our students walk around school with serious faces and chips on their shoulders, then they have most definitely missed the heart of God. We must help our students see that there is much more good in the world than there is evil. Our students should enjoy life—and be enjoyable!

4. Accepting

In at least nine places in the Gospels, Jesus is shown sharing a meal with a person or group of people other than his disciples. Interestingly, in seven of those nine times, Jesus is eating with people who were considered the worst sinners of their day. Tax collectors. Prostitutes. Only twice do we see him eating with religious people. What does that tell you about the personality of Christ?

If there is a characteristic that Jesus exemplified more than any other, it is acceptance. Jesus was always befriending people who had shady or difficult pasts. He was always accepting of people who others considered socially or relationally off-limits.

We will spend an entire chapter embracing the idea of unconditional acceptance. It's a major thread that weaves its way throughout the pages of this book. Understanding this aspect of Jesus' personality is critical for our students. They need to realize: People will gravitate toward people and environments that are accepting, and they will shy away from people and environments that convey rejection.

The closest that unbelieving teenagers in our cities are going to get to Jesus is our core students. They are the church—and they are meant to reflect the authentic, relevant, enjoyable, and accepting personality and purpose of Christ.

Preparing Students for the Influential Life

To do this effectively, they must have Christ's perspective.

Not long ago Stuart told me that he's getting bored with roller coasters. It probably has to do with being a parent *and* a youth pastor: He frequents amusement parks and rides roller coasters so often that he knows what to expect. On a roller coaster, it is the unexpected that causes your stomach to visit your throat and ask to be excused. It is the unknown that somehow convinces your bladder it needs to empty itself just before you take off. It's the best part!

But Stuart has grown so accustomed to amusement-park rides that he always knows what's going to happen next. The thrill is gone.

Or at least it was.

Recently Stuart met "The Incredible Hulk" at Universal Studios in Orlando, Florida, and his innocence returned—at least for the first ride. Here's what he told me:

> Up to that point, every roller coaster I had ever conquered had the traditional *click-click-click* climb time before you reached the top, saw the expanse below, and began the descent into chaos. Not so with the Hulk. In the middle of the *click-click-click*, with no warning at all, you are launched forward at breakneck speed into the unknown. The sudden thrust is unexpected. You have no time to gain your bearings. It scared me senseless. I had to change pants.
>
> But after the first time, I knew what to expect, and

the fear dissipated. In fact, after my initial Hulk encounter, I purposely tried to sit with teens who had never ridden the Hulk before. Especially hysterical were the reactions of the "tough guys" who were under the impression that they were God's gift to the female gender. I would strike up the same conversation with each of them as we began the *click-click-click:*

"Dude, have you been on this before?"

"Nope."

"You scared?" (The clicks start.)

"Me? No way! I love roller coasters. This ain't nothin' but"—(sudden launch)—"OOOOHHHHH AAAAAHHHHH!"

Now that's entertainment!

Not So Funny

Of course, it's not humorous at all when this same thing happens to students who are launched into Max Q. There is nothing funny about teenagers being thrown into a spiral of spiritual apathy and depression because they didn't understand the magnitude of the task of making disciples. This is not entertainment. This is war. For far too long, we in youth ministry have sent "babies" into this war and then been surprised when they've come back wounded, traumatized, and limping. "How could this happen?" we ask.

It happens for the same reason we lose control on a roller coaster we have never experienced before: Our students don't know what awaits them.

Remember the gauntlet from chapter 1? Knowing what lies ahead diminishes our potential of being thrown off (or worse). It helps us to remain in control and not be swept away by intimidation and fear. It enables us to be prepared so we can respond correctly in the midst of the chaos.

If you and I are to develop students of influence—students who can withstand the forces of spiritual Max Q—then we need to tell them what to expect. They cannot enter maximum dynamic pressure under false pretenses or with naïve assumptions. NASA astronauts would never do that; their lives are at stake. Neither should our students. Their spiritual lives and testimonies are at stake. Their very lives may be at stake. Yes, the creative, regenerative power of the universe lives in them, but that does not diminish the pressure of a culture and mindset that whistles past at a fearfully intimidating velocity and pitch.

What the Future Holds

Jesus understood this. John 15:18–20 records a conversation Christ had with his disciples to prepare them for what was ahead as they began the process of disciplism:

> If the world hates you, keep in mind that it hated me first. If you belonged to the world, it would love you as its own. As it is, you do not belong to the world, but I have chosen you out of the world. That is why the world hates you. Remember the words I spoke to you: "No servant is greater than his master." If they persecuted me, they will persecute you also. If they obeyed my teaching, they will obey yours also.

Jesus told the disciples what they could expect. And he definitely didn't sugarcoat it. In fact, he seemed to imply that rejection and making disciples are synonymous terms. He continued:

> All this I have told you so that you will not go astray. They will put you out of the synagogue; in fact, a time is coming when anyone who kills you will think he is offering a service to God. They will do such things because they have not known the Father or me. I have told you this, so that when the time comes you will remember that I warned you. (John 16:1–4)

Jesus didn't want the disciples to go forward under false pretenses, naïvely assuming that making disciples would be easy. He didn't want them to be surprised and thrown off track by what surely lay ahead. Rather, he wanted them to anticipate rejection and ridicule, so that when they encountered it, they wouldn't have to surrender to it. So he told them the truth: that people who didn't know Christ would have a radically different perspective on life from those who did—so much so that unbelievers would think they were doing God a favor by killing a disciple.

The same principles that Jesus laid out for the disciples hold true for our students. Teenagers who attempt to live godly lives before their peers will face rejection and ridicule. If they begin to invest their lives into the lives of unbelieving friends, there is a strong possibility they will encounter resistance at the very least—and often much worse.

That's because the perspective of their lost friends on

much of life is radically different from their own. Their friends view faith, relationships, the opposite sex, choices, parents, authority figures, even themselves, through a frame of reference that promotes self as God. It's as if they're looking through the big end of a telescope to see the world: Everything reduces to self.

The interesting thing about this postmodern student culture is that the majority of teenagers claim to be tolerant of most ideologies and philosophies—that is, as long as those philosophies don't threaten their own personal belief systems. If a system of standards threatens them, tolerance and acceptance go out the window. For our students to begin to live the Christ-life before them is threatening. It flips the telescope, causing them to see themselves in reality.

Our students will be rejected. Count on it. If every path has a predetermined destination, then one of the stops on the path to influence is rejection. Why? Because when Jesus ascended to heaven, the plan he set in place to redeem mankind depended upon men and women living out authentic Christian lives before lost and needy people. The Holy Spirit will use our students' lives to convict their unbelieving peers. That's been God's plan all along.

What will be their friends' reaction when they begin to sense that they are wrong or don't measure up? Most likely it *won't* be to admit it. Our natural human tendency is to deny or reject the standard by which we're being judged. Think about it. If you were convinced that you weighed 200 pounds and you got on a scale that said you weighed 225 pounds, what would be your immediate reaction? If you're normal, you would think that the scale was wrong (denial). Or you would get angry at the scale and want to throw it away (rejection). You would swear that there was something wrong with the scale, not your weight.

Our students must understand that their very presence will be a constant reminder to their unbelieving peers of everything those peers are not. If our students are living lives that demonstrate godly standards, right priorities, accountability, and unconditional acceptance (as we will discuss in the chapters that follow), then the "scale" is going to seem wacky to their lost friends. And just as overweight people are constantly reminded by a scale of their actual size, those friends are going to be reminded of their true state every time our students are around. Our Christian students are the scales that give an accurate picture of who lost teenagers really are—and are not.

Standing Up and Sticking Out

A teenager who stands up for his or her convictions is going to stick out. In a culture that believes there are no moral absolutes and that all standards are relative, it is not difficult for such a student to get the attention of unbelievers.

We're reminded of the story of Shadrach, Meshach, and Abednego in the book of Daniel. You know the details: King Nebuchadnezzar had laid siege to Jerusalem and captured it. Then he'd chosen the finest of the Israelite young men—the All-American types—for training in the Babylonian way and the king's service. Three of these young men were named Shadrach, Meshach, and Abednego. These three guys loved

God with all their hearts, yet they still found favor in the eyes of Nebuchadnezzar.

One day, in his arrogance, King Nebuchadnezzar decided to build a huge image of gold that all of Babylon would have to bow down to in a demonstration of loyalty to the king. The image was constructed, the command was given, the band started playing, and people throughout the kingdom started bowing—everyone except Shadrach, Meshach, and Abednego.

These three stuck out like a sore thumb. All because they just . . . stood.

Our students live in a modern-day Babylon. Everyone is bowing to *something* other than the one true God. In such an environment, our teens don't have to be All-Americans to get attention; they don't have to be prom queens or star football players to have influence. What made Shadrach, Meshach, and Abednego stick out was not the fact that they were impressive in appearance or stature. The truth is, it's not hard to look impressive when you're standing up and everyone else is bowing down!

Daniel 3:13 tells us that Nebuchadnezzar became "furious with rage" at the three Israelites. Sometimes simply standing for something is all it takes to cause others to become belligerent and angry! Our students need to understand this. But the king's anger didn't move Shadrach, Meshach, and Abednego. They stayed faithful, opening the door for Nebuchadnezzar to ask questions about their faith and giving them a golden opportunity to tell the king about their God.

The same opportunities will come to our students. Their

faithfulness will eventually be questioned. It will also be tested. Nebuchadnezzar tested the three young men by throwing them in a fiery furnace. Our students can expect to face their own "fiery furnaces" as their unbelieving friends test them too.

All because they stand while everyone else is bowing down!

Rejection Is a Good Thing

Many times students have come to us and said, "My friends don't listen to me. They criticize me and make fun of me." Our response has always been the same: "Are you so determined to be right that you are offending them with your comments and actions? If that's the case, you need to back off and stop answering questions your friends aren't asking. But if you're not being pushy and your friends are still rejecting and ridiculing you, then you are on the right track, and God is at work.

"It is far better to be hated than ignored. It is far better to be left out than to be included, if inclusion means compromise. You can't be a hero in the eyes of the world and in the eyes of God as well. Those concepts are like oil and water: They don't mix."

No one likes being rejected. It's certainly not the reaction our students are hoping for. But rejection doesn't necessarily mean failure when it comes to being influential. It's no reason for our students to get depressed. On the contrary, rejection can mean that something is actually "connecting." It can mean that they are beginning to reflect Jesus.

Reasons for Rejection

In the chapters that follow, we will show you how to help your students stay connected while they battle the emotional burden of rejection. The first key is this: understanding that Jesus, two thousand years before any of us stepped foot in a youth group, warned that we would be rejected for his name's sake.

The second key is understanding the three main reasons unbelieving teens reject Christian students who live godly lives before them:

1. Our students are foreigners.

Speaking to his disciples only hours before his betrayal and arrest, Jesus said, "If you belonged to the world, it would love you as its own. As it is, you do not belong to the world, but I have chosen you out of the world. That is why the world hates you" (John 15:19).

Notice that Jesus begins with an interesting observation. He says that if we as Christ-followers belonged to the world, then we would be loved by the world. In other words, if our students were like everyone else in their high school, then they would be accepted as such. But his point is clear: As followers of Christ, our teenagers are not like everyone else. They are "aliens." They are like E.T. walking through the school halls. They stick out like Marilyn Manson at a George Strait concert.

It's human nature for people with common ideas and common attitudes to find each other. Look around any junior high or high school and you will see this dynamic in action. Smart kids gravitate to smart kids, jocks gravitate to jocks, skaters to skaters, cheerleader-types to cheerleader-types, and the list goes on. When you add a student who has placed his or her faith and trust in Christ to the mix, it's like setting an immovable buoy in the middle of a fast-flowing undertow of common attitude.

2. Unbelievers don't have a relationship with Christ.

Jesus continued: "They will do such things because they have not known the Father or me" (John 16:3).

Why do lost teenagers reject our students? This issue is lack of relationship, not lack of information. Unbelievers don't believe that Jesus is who he claimed to be. Or they believe, but they have never trusted in him or submitted their lives to him. The whole idea of submitting to Christ—of placing their lives under the authority of an invisible God—seems incomprehensible and threatening.

Rejection, then, is the result of unbelieving students not knowing Jesus. Our students become guilty simply by association.

3. The Holy Spirit is at work convicting others through our students.

This part of Jesus' charge to his disciples is a bit more seeker-*un*friendly:

When he [the Holy Spirit] comes, he will convict the world of guilt in regard to sin and righteousness and judgment: in regard to sin, because men do not believe

57

in me; in regard to righteousness, because I am going to the Father, where you can see me no longer; and in regard to judgment, because the prince of this world now stands condemned. (John 16:8–11)

We have touched on this point before. Students who are living in the freedom and grace found only in faith in Christ will be a walking illustration to their peers—a constant demonstration and reminder to their friends of their desperate need for forgiveness and a savior. Through our students, the Holy Spirit will communicate the fact that Christianity is not a behavioral balancing act or a matter of making sure your good deeds outweigh the bad ones. No, Christianity is based totally on what Christ did for us, not what we do for him.

When our students live out the Christ-life before their peers, the barrier that separates sinful teenagers from a holy God will grow increasingly evident to them. Our students do not have to continually berate their peers about sinful habits or lifestyles. What will cause sin to become more noticeable will be the striking contrast between a compromised life and the life of freedom in Christ.

The picture of righteousness our students represent is threatening to unbelieving teens. That's why they sometimes practically beg our students to sin. They exert a constant, never-ending cascade of Max Q: "Come on, just one drink . . . just one drag . . . just one sniff." We've had many of our core students come to us and ask, "Why can't they just drop it already?" Why? Because our students are everything their lost peers know they could and should be—and they hate the comparison! Our students are like a brother or sister who always does things right. They are an ever-constant standard of rightness that can't be explained away or ignored.

Deep inside, unbelieving students know there must be an accounting for sin and lack of rightness with God. To them, our students are like an alarm clock that goes off at the same time every morning. They hate the shrill *ring-ring-ring*. They may hit the snooze button over and over. But they know that sooner or later, they're going to have to get up.

Which teenagers will reject our students the most vehemently? Not those pagan friends who have never stepped foot in church, whose lives are in complete shambles. No, the most intense rejection will come from those students who grew up in church and have since abandoned it. It will come from those teens who have experienced enough of religion to make them wary and skeptical. It will come from those who have seen the worst in people and mistakenly connect their bad experiences with God.

We need to warn our students: Jesus was rejected. So were the disciples. They will be too.

The Promise of Peace

All this talk of rejection could seem to be grounds for frustration and discouragement. Our students may ask, "Is influence worth the cost?" Max Q is tough enough; with a big heap of rejection added in, it may seem unbearable.

We need to remind our students (and ourselves) of Jesus' promise in John 14:27: "Peace I leave with you; my peace I give you." Jesus doesn't promise us a storm-free life; he promises us peace in the midst of every storm. And biblical faith is riveted in believing that God is who he says he is and that he will do what he has promised to do. His promises are like a bridge that carries our students from being people of wishful thinking to believers of mountainlike faith.

In the same verse, Jesus explained, "I do not give to you as the world gives." In other words, the peace Jesus gives is not based on the usual things, like circumstances or how we feel. No, God's peace is similar to joy; it is an unswerving condition of the soul. Our students can walk in boldness and courage, knowing that a peace that simply does not make sense to the world—God's peace—will set up a protective guard around their emotions.

Christian students who have an overwhelming sense of peace—a peace that fortifies them and helps them maintain healthy emotions in the midst of chaos—have the potential to become extremely influential. These are the students who will stay in the fire. These are the students who will not flinch when all hell breaks loose around them. Few of our students experience this kind of peace, mainly because they retreat from adversity so fast that God never has an opportunity to prove himself.

The truth is, whatever comes against our students has passed first through the powerful, yet permitting, hands of Abba Father—Daddy. Loving, caring fathers may allow their children to experience difficulty and hardship, but they will not allow them to be totally destroyed. To have an all-powerful, all-knowing, always-present God for a heavenly Father is not something to be taken lightly or for granted.

On the contrary, our students can bank their very existence on their relationship with him. And in the midst of trouble, they can experience peace.

Several years ago I heard a story about a father who took his elementary-age son and daughter fishing on the Tombigbee Intercoastal Waterway in south Alabama. They had been fishing many times together, and the father had taught his children all the intricacies of fishing and boating safety. They had discussed many times what to do if trouble ever found them.

And on this day, trouble did.

As was their custom, the father and his children put their boat in at a landing and began to make their way out of the small tributary into the river. The Tombigbee Waterway is used by numerous industries for transporting products, so there are always huge barges and tugboats on the waterway. With the father sitting at the steering wheel and his son and daughter sitting behind him, they began to dodge the floating logs and trash as well as the other, much larger, vessels.

Suddenly, in the wake of a passing barge, the boat began to rock. The father shouted over his shoulder for his kids to hold on. But the little boat was hardly a match for the pounding water; and the boat began to toss back and forth more violently, heavy logs and other trash in the waterway beating against its sides.

Finally, after what seemed like an eternity, they reached calmer waters. The father looked back to his right to make sure his son was OK. The boy was obviously shaken but fine. Then he turned and looked back to his left.

His little girl was not in the boat.

His eyes darted frantically to the water. There was his daughter's life vest, floating away—but his little girl was not in it. He began to scream her name, searching the muddy water for any sign of her. Nothing.

In the madness of the moment, it occurred to the father that if his little girl had been tossed out of the boat, she would have fallen into the water near the outboard motor. In the split second that this thought ran through his mind, the motor suddenly shut off. The father's heart dropped: *She has fallen into the propeller*.

He rushed to the back of the boat and looked down into the water behind the motor, expecting to see a horrific sight of blood and torn flesh.

What he saw instead was his little girl's face—just below the surface of the water—smiling up at him. The sweatshirt she had been wearing was entangled in the prop, and she couldn't surface.

The father turned to his son to ask for a knife to cut the girl loose. His son was already there, holding the knife he wanted, knowingly extending it to him before he even asked. Quickly the father cut the sweatshirt away from the motor and pulled his daughter into the boat. For a long time, he held her and wept. Her sweatshirt was torn, but she did not have as much as a scratch.

When he finally regained his composure, the father asked his daughter how she could have been smiling when she was under the water in such a desperate situation.

"You taught us what to do in case of trouble," she responded. "I knew you would come and get me. I had nothing to be afraid of."

May the peace of God, which transcends all understanding, guard our students' hearts and minds in Christ Jesus!

Pressure Points

1. Why would a student gravitate to your church and ministry? Does your answer have to do more with programs and facilities or with people?

2. What are you doing to develop students that emulate the personality of Christ? What is your greatest challenge in this effort?

3. Consider this statement: "Knowing what lies ahead diminishes our potential of being thrown off (or worse). It helps us to remain in control and not be swept away by intimidation and fear. It enables us to be prepared so we can respond correctly in the midst of the chaos." Do your students recognize and understand the seriousness of the Max Q that lies ahead for them? If not, why not?

4. What do you consider to be the major characteristics of an influential student?

5. How did Jesus exemplify influence in the midst of rejection?

He who thinks he leads
but has no followers
is only taking a walk.

JOHN MAXWELL

3

Understanding Influence

The Connection between Social Science and the Gospel

When U.S. Special Forces commandos attempted to rescue American prisoners from the infamous Hanoi Hilton prison during the Vietnam War, the operation was conducted almost without flaw. The commandos trained in great secrecy for weeks in advance. When the day finally came, the commando team quickly took control of the prison. The team was in and out and safely back at a U.S. base before enemy forces could respond.

Their only real flaw in the mission had to do with intelligence. Shortly before the raid, a remote-controlled drone was sent to collect information. During an in-flight turn, the drone banked slightly, causing its cameras to point toward the sky for a brief moment. As a result, the drone failed to capture imagery that would have revealed that the Hanoi Hilton prisoners had been moved. There were no prisoners to free from the Hanoi Hilton on that particular day.

How Do You Define Success?

Was the mission successful? It depends on how the planners defined success. If the mission was to take control of the Hanoi Hilton, then the mission was successful. If the mission was to boost morale among American troops—especially those being held in other prisons—then the mission was successful. And if the mission was to demonstrate that the United States was willing and able to conduct these kinds of operations, then the mission was successful. But if the mission was to free the prisoners who had been in the Hanoi Hilton, then the mission failed.[1]

In many ways, this real-life story painfully corresponds with our efforts as youth leaders to reach an unbelieving generation of teens with the truth. Our array of programs, events, and environments for reaching students is vast. We work tirelessly to make sure that these components are energized, full of life, and able to connect to the hearts and lives of unbelieving students. Our means to free the "prisoners" are strategic, effective, and full of power.

But here's the question: Are we being successful in our mission? Like the Hanoi Hilton rescue, it depends on how we define success. If our mission is to design creative environments, then many of us are successful. If our mission is to show the church that the youth ministry cares about lost students, then most of us are successful. And if our mission is to provide an alternative to the world's idea of fun and games, then we are probably successful again.

If our mission is to influence lost teenagers with the gospel, however, then most of us would have to admit our mission is not being accomplished. We are failing. More times than not, there are few, if any, "prisoners" that need to be freed in our youth-ministry environments. The cool and relevant programs and settings we've worked so hard to develop in order to impact lost students are being filled to capacity with our own core students and their Christian friends from other churches.

If you and I are content to fill our environments with Christian students, then we have a problem. We will never influence unbelieving students for Christ. Reggie Joiner, North Point's family-ministries pastor, says this:

> Conventional methods of evaluating success have given us false indicators about what is really happening. The number of programs, an increase in our budget, and beating last year's record can convince us that we are gaining ground. One of the great indicators of relevance is what is happening relationally with our people. Jesus had a reputation of always making people more important than what was on the agenda or program. At times, he frustrated his disciples, and it always threatened the Pharisees.[2]

In other words, our standard of success must not be centered on statistical goals and data. It must be centered on relationships. People must take priority over programs—even if this means frustrating a few folks.

Influence is about people. It is a function of connected lives. For this reason, in order to reach the unbelieving teenagers in our communities, we must help our core students grasp the nuances of person-to-person influence. By understanding the social science of influence, they will be better equipped to spiritually influence their peers for the sake of Christ.

God's Plan of Influence

Before we go on, let's establish a few things up front so there's no misunderstanding: We absolutely believe that God alone is the agent of change and the giver of life. Neither we nor our students can rejuvenate a dead sinful nature. Only God can raise the dead. He chooses to move when he chooses to move, because he is God. We have no control over what he does or does not do. To have that control would make us God.

Furthermore, we believe that God can and often has bypassed the need for a relational bridge and a redeemed people to reach lost souls. Stories of his direct intervention in people's lives are mind-boggling and so inspiring! We always want our students to believe in and pray to a God who can do the impossible. He has proven himself in this regard time and time again.

But we also believe that what our students have the capacity to do within the scope of God's plan, they need to be enabled to do well. Developing influential students means that we enable our students to become exceptional relational bridge builders. And becoming effective relational bridge builders means that our students not only understand the role of God and his Spirit in reaching lost people but also the principles that govern what makes people tick. There are facts about human nature and the human psyche that are powerful and shouldn't be ignored. If our students' role is to influence their peers for Christ (aren't we all, as Christians, to know God and *make him known?*), it only makes sense that they understand how social science and the gospel connect.

Weird Science

The word *influence* is really an overarching term. Within it are several submeanings that make up the whole. Basically, any time a person deliberately attempts to change another person's thoughts, feelings, or behavior—either through verbal or nonverbal communication—he or she is exerting influence.

Whether or not the second person actually changes as a result of that influence depends upon many things, including his or her *attitude*. Attitude is dependent upon a person's internal evaluation of an object or thought. Everyone in life holds up an evaluative tape measure (good to bad) and measures people, objects, concepts, and things against that scale. For example, what's your attitude on:

Atlanta Braves baseball: good or bad?

Squeezing toothpaste from the middle of the tube: good or bad?

Saddam Hussein: good or bad?

God: good or bad?

Your evaluation of these topics reveals your attitude or heart about them. That attitude provides your behavior with fuel for its fire. It keeps you moving in a certain direction. It is why you do what you do. Your heart determines your actions.

How does this play into the student culture? All teenagers have some evaluation, some picture, of who God is and what he is like. They have their own formulated attitude toward God. If they have a picture of God that is small or nonexistent, then that picture will drive their attitude, and they will be ambivalent or even antagonistic toward the idea of God. If their picture of God is huge and powerful and loving, however, then their attitude will drive them to live a life of passion for God.

The goal of our core students (the ones with the big picture of God) is to influence the attitude of their unbelieving friends (the ones with the small or nonexistent picture). It's to persuade them to change their evaluation of God. The goal is heart change, because the heart drives behavior. Christianity is not about behavior modification anyway. It is about a change of heart. Jesus said it this way when challenged by the Pharisees about his disciples' behavior: "Don't you see that whatever enters the mouth goes into the stomach and then out of the body? But the things that come out of the mouth come from the heart, and these make a man 'unclean'" (Matthew 15:17–18).

In other words, what comes out of your mouth marks you. What comes out of your mouth originated in your heart; your heart, then, launches your words and actions.

As youth leaders we have a propensity to focus our energies on changing a teenager's behavior. We even decide a particular student is in need of influence based on our judgment of his or her behavior. But it is the heart that is the real issue.

To affect behavior we have to affect the heart. It must be the object of our influence. But there is more. After we figure out how to influence the heart of a lost student, we must figure out how to make the student *use* that heart. First get the heart change. Then get the heart to drive behavior. (Sounds like disciplism to me.)

Working with God

Of course, as we've already said, God is the only agent of true change of the heart. But there are a lot of different ways we—and our students—can work with God as he accomplishes what only he can do. It helps if we understand the two major factors that cause the heart to drive behavior: *attitude availability* and *attitude relevance*. If a given attitude is available (in close proximity, accessible), then it's more likely to drive behavior. If a given attitude is relevant (useful or applicable) then it, too, is more likely to drive behavior.

Attitude Availability

An attitude is available when we can think of it, when we're aware that we've got a particular attitude on a topic, and when that attitude is "turned on," so to speak. We can actually increase the likelihood that another person will have a desired attitude available and turned on by doing what social scientists call "priming." Essentially, priming is a setup activity. We do something that gets the other person fired up or poised to think about a particular topic in a certain way.

Consider an extremely hypothetical example. Let's say you

want a teenage boy to have a horrible attitude about his girl-friend's attractiveness. You can "prime" him by showing him pictures of a supermodel or someone else's drop-dead gor-geous girlfriend. If you want him to have a good attitude toward his girlfriend's attractiveness, however, you can prime him by having him look at pictures of relatively ugly girls. The priming task of viewing pictures activates his attitudes about the concept of attractiveness. Later, when you ask that teen to make a judgment about his girlfriend, those primed attitudes will be available to guide his behavior (and drive how he rates his girlfriend).

If our students want to be influential in the lives of their unbelieving friends, they have to "prime" them by giving them a living picture of who God is and the difference he can make in their lives. Their priming task is to live radical lives characterized by passion for Christ and compassion for their lost friends—in close enough proximity to their friends for the picture to be seen. Then when God prompts those unbelieving friends to make a judgment about his son, Jesus Christ, the primed attitudes will be available to guide their behavior and drive how they respond to the person of Jesus.

If you've ever lived in the country and had to depend on a well for running water, you probably know about "priming the pump." These days the pumps on most wells are motor-ized and run on electricity. But that doesn't mean they're trouble-free. Invariably, the pump stops working at some inconvenient time, and you have to go out and prime the pump. Growing up, Stuart often had to take a gallon milk jug full of water out to his family's pump and pour the water into a certain spot, in hopes that the pump would remember what to do, kick back on, and start pumping water again from the well. He would have to make trip after trip with his gallon jug of water to prime the pump. It was a time-consuming and painstaking process. Basically what he was doing was painting a "picture" to the pump—so that the pump would develop an "attitude" about pumping water—so that it might develop a "behavior" of pumping water from the well.

In many ways that's what our students must do: prime the heart-pumps of their lost friends. They must get close enough to pour "living water" into their lost friends' lives so that those friends develop a positive attitude toward the water and begin to want it for themselves. Our students must give their friends an accurate picture of God to replace the faulty pictures that have influenced their attitudes and driven their behaviors to that point.

After all, isn't that why God came to earth and existed in a body: to prime mankind's pump by demonstrating in the flesh what God is like? The apostle John, the one Jesus loved, said this about God's priming: "The Word became flesh and made his dwelling among us. We have seen his glory, the glory of the One and Only, who came from the Father, full of grace and truth" (John 1:14).

We want to emphasize one point, however: Students don't have to spend tons of time and energy priming their friends to have bad attitudes toward their own sin. Rather, they need to spend that time and energy living the Christ-life of love and painting a beautiful picture of God for their friends. The contrast will speak for itself.

Attitude Relevance

An attitude is relevant when it applies to the situation at hand. We in youth ministry are notorious for answering questions that lost teenagers are not asking. We try to force God into places that students could care less about. Or we make the grave mistake of majoring in minors. Or we package the truth—a truth that is the same yesterday, today, and forever—in such an irrelevant way that students become bored and apathetic toward it.

Earlier in this chapter, we mentioned an encounter Jesus had with the Pharisees and teachers of the law over his disciples' behavior. Do you know what the Pharisees were angry with the disciples about? Poor hygiene habits! "Why do your disciples break the tradition of the elders?" they said. "They don't wash their hands before they eat!" (Matthew 15:2).

How irrelevant is that? What in the world does not washing your hands before you eat have to do with eternity? With God? It's absurd!

This is where Jesus is such a great example to us. He took an irrelevant question and made a more than relevant connection. He knew the real issue in this situation was the Pharisees' hearts—not a lack of Wet Wipes. So he took a timeless truth and made it relate to people in that situation.

Likewise, our students need to learn how to take the truth and make it relevant to their unbelieving friends' lives. Just because they're Christians doesn't mean our students have to be relationally retarded and culturally ignorant. Our enemy is not the culture. Our enemy is not MTV. Our nemesis is not

Eminem. The real enemy is a distorted picture of who God is and what he is like.

A friend of ours, Travis Crim, lives in Los Angeles, California. Travis is there to help students assimilate into the Hollywood culture and become spiritually influential in the arena of entertainment. Recently, on the set of a particular movie, Travis met an aspiring actress who was raised in a religious home but had pretty much turned away from God due to over-zealous parents and a legalistic church. Since that initial contact, Travis and his wife, Delaine, have been steadily building a relationship of trust with this girl, going out to dinner from time to time and having lengthy conversations in their home about spirituality and God.

When Travis and Delaine invited this young lady to church with them one Sunday, she surprised them by accepting their invitation. Fortunately, Travis and Delaine are involved in one of the most creative and relevant churches in the country. Their pastor was in the middle of a teaching series discussing three different movies and their implications on culture from a Christian perspective. The film being reviewed that particular Sunday was *The Shawshank Redemption*, which just happened to be one of this girl's favorites. The stage was set up in full Siskel-and-Ebert style, with the pastor and his associate exchanging insightful commentary. Theme-oriented worship music and movie clips were intermingled throughout.

God spoke directly to this girl that Sunday. During the entire service, she continued to nod her head and give non-verbal affirmation to what she was hearing. Travis almost expected to see her jump out of her seat and shout, "Amen!" Can you imagine: God was speaking to her through a movie—in church! After the service this young lady told Travis and Delaine that she wished she'd met them and found the church earlier. She also said she was going to bring her ex-fiancé to the following Sunday's service in which *The Matrix*—one of his favorite movies—was going to be reviewed.

If teenagers can find nothing relevant to base a positive attitude toward Christ on, it doesn't matter what we or our students say or do. Attitudes will drive behavior when they are relevant to the situation.

Attitude Is Not Enough

So all we have to do is produce the right attitude change in teenagers; and forever onward those teens will show the desired attitude-driven behavior, right? If we throw ourselves into events that prompt heart change, get students to walk to the front and make a public response to God, then our job is done, right? Wrong. Attitude change is not enough. We can't ignore the process of connecting a new heart to a new life. The world is littered with students who gave signs of heart change without following through with behavior change. They never developed heart-to-behavior consistency.

Mere attitude change is not sufficient to guarantee behavior change. More often than not, the process of personal renewal takes time. Receiving a regenerated heart and a new identity in Christ happens in an instant; it's an occasion. Having that new heart affect behavior, however, typically doesn't happen overnight; it's a process.

This is the idea that flows from Paul's challenge in Romans 12:2 to not conform any longer to the "Me first!" system of this world but to be changed by the renewing of our minds. Our students have to do more than prime the pump. They must go beyond ensuring attitude availability and attitude relevance. Once God uses our students to capture the hearts of their lost friends, then influence is needed to help those friends develop heart-to-behavior consistency.

Principles of Influence

No two students are alike, of course. But most teenagers are influenced to one degree or another by the following five principles:

1. The Principle of Comparison

Has this ever happened to you? You are walking down the street when you notice just ahead of you three or four people standing on the street corner, looking straight up in the air. As you move in closer to them, what do you do? You look up in the air. Is it a bird? Is it a plane? Is it Superman?

No, it's the principle of comparison. When others are doing something, we think we should do it too. We compare our behavior against the standard of what everybody else is doing; and if we notice a discrepancy between our actions and what we observe in others, we change.

Our students capitalize on this principle of influence when their lives are an obviously different alternative to the normal lives being lived by the majority. Our students need to ask themselves: How does my life compare to those around me?

And as youth leaders we need to ask: What distinguishes my students from others? Is there any noticeable difference— something that would cause an unbeliever to compare his or her life to theirs?

Peter paints the picture this way in a letter he wrote to Jewish and gentile Christians scattered abroad. Interestingly, he wrote this letter from Babylon, a center of paganism:

> Dear friends, I urge you, as aliens and strangers in the world, to abstain from sinful desires, which war against your soul. Live such good lives among the pagans that, though they accuse you of doing wrong, they may see your good deeds and glorify God on the day he visits us. (1 Peter 2:11–12)

The Greek word used for *see* in verse 12 means "careful watching over a period of time." The idea communicated here is that we as Christians are to live such God-centered lives of goodness—doing deeds that can be seen by all as good—that over time people who've been observing our lives will evaluate their own lives in comparison and make the choice to live for God. They won't be making a snap judgment, but rather an educated decision based on the leverage of our lives.

2. The Principle of Likability

It's a simple truth that we are open to the influence of people we like. Very few of us do anything modeled or suggested by people we disdain. Think of it this way: Would you rather buy a product endorsed by Michael Jordan or Saddam Hussein? Enough said. In our culture likability equals leverage.

At one time Stuart's wife, Kellee, sold Premier Designs jewelry. What happens at a Premier Designs jewelry party? People who know each other come over to the house of a mutual friend. Everybody eats a little. Everybody chats a bit. Everybody has a little fun. Then the mutual friend steps up and introduces a new person, who then breaks out the product: Premier Designs jewelry.

"Wow, isn't that new person friendly? Isn't the jewelry pretty?" Everybody smiles, everybody laughs, and usually everybody buys something.

Of course, Premier is not the only product sold in this way. Mary Kay Cosmetics has pushed a lot of powder and given away a lot of pink Cadillacs through the principle of likability. You can probably think of a few other businesses to add to this list. The basis of the sale is the fact that the buyer likes somebody involved in the transaction—the salesperson, the hostess, the friend sitting in the next chair who just bought fifty dollars worth of lipstick. (It's a safe bet that the principle of comparison is also in operation.)

Apparently Jesus spent time nurturing this principle. Luke 2:52 tells us "Jesus grew in wisdom and stature, and in favor with God and men." This verse serves as the bridge between Jesus as a child and Jesus as a man. It is no coincidence that part of his development related to finding favor with people. He developed likability!

God doesn't intend for our students to be boring, stoic,

judgmental robots. Nowhere does the Bible imply that Christianity equals relational retardation. Our students capitalize on the principle of likability when they live open, joyful lives. Christian students should always be the life of the party. (Jesus was.) They know the Creator of the universe personally. What better reason to enjoy life!

3. The Principle of Authority

When you consider someone an authority in a certain area, you are more likely to believe what that person says or endorses. That's why Michael Jordan can sell oodles of basketball shoes.

You may be old enough to remember the TV series *Marcus Welby, M.D.* The lead actor, Robert Young, portrayed a friendly, wise, and incredibly available physician who never lost a patient (except when it would increase the show's Nielsen ratings).

Interestingly, Robert Young transitioned his fame as Dr. Marcus Welby into a very productive sideline. He sold aspirin on TV ads—not as Robert Young, the actor, but as Dr. Marcus Welby. It didn't matter to consumers that his character was fictional. Robert Young looked and acted like an authority. And sales of his brand of aspirin increased. Why? Because when a source is considered an authority, we feel like we can believe it.

Students who leverage this principle are those students who are committed to excellence in whatever they do. We will explore this idea more in the chapter on sustained influence. But the bottom line is, teenagers reserve a place of influence for people they respect and consider good at whatever it is they do. That's why a student who is a gifted athlete or a brilliant thinker can influence other students on campus. Competence breeds authority, and authority breeds influence.

4. The Principle of Reciprocity

You're walking down the street, minding your own business, when a stranger approaches from the opposite direction. The stranger makes eye contact with you and smiles. If you are like most people, you automatically respond with a smile of your own as you pass the stranger and continue down the street.

A stranger gives you something (a smile) and you give back something in return (a smile). A nice way to meet people, but what does this have to do with influence?

Simple: We have a tendency to think that if someone gives us something and we accept it, we are now obligated to give something back. That's the principle behind our infamous youth-ministry pizza blasts. We entice students to come and chow down on all the free pizza they can eat. Then, once they've had their fill, we ask them to sit and listen to a speaker talk about the gospel. In other words: "We gave you something; now you give us something back."

Our students have to be careful not to abuse the principle of reciprocity. Expecting a return on a relational investment as it relates to spiritual influence can be dangerous. We have so abused this principle in our churches and youth ministries that many students don't trust Christians anymore.

Our students must learn to love their lost peers with no expectation of reciprocity—no strings attached. Unconditional love is like a giant heart magnet. God tells us, "I have loved you with an everlasting love; I have drawn you with loving-kindness" (Jeremiah 31:3). The apostle Paul says that "God's kindness leads you toward repentance" (Romans 2:4). A heart simply can't resist true kindness and unconditional love. It's virtually impossible. If our students love their friends uncon-ditionally, they will use the leverage of reciprocity without abusing it. And they will gain a degree of influence among their peers that will stand the test of time and pressure.

5. The Principle of Scarcity

Rare things are highly valued in our society. Consider how much money the record-setting homerun baseballs of Mark McGuire and Barry Bonds have been auctioned for. And what makes a diamond so valuable? If there were hundreds of thousands of diamonds in the world, would they be as expen-sive? No, their scarcity is what gives them extremely high value. We assume that if something is rare, it is good.

How does this principle connect with our students? Students who live by godly standards are rare in our society. Teenagers who make the name and fame of God the priority of their lives are like rare jewels. Unfortunately, our youth ministries produce far too many students who resemble those candy rings that kids love to buy at the candy store. The "dia-mond" looks big and pretty, but it's just sugar. A sweet-crazed five-year-old can reduce it to nothing in three minutes.

Today's student culture needs Christian students who are willing to be rare pearls and sparkling diamonds among their peers. Their value and influence can be immeasurable. As

Solomon wrote, "Gold there is, and rubies in abundance, but lips that speak knowledge are a rare jewel" (Proverbs 20:15).

Why These Principles Work—and Why They Don't

These principles of influence work because the thought processes of most teenagers are somewhat lazy or heuristic in nature. By "heuristic," we mean that students tend to lean on feelings, preferences, and emotions as the basis for their attitudes. Tolerance, relative thinking, and puberty all contribute to this preference for the heuristic mode. If something *feels* right, then students can be easily influenced by it—even if it doesn't make sense.[3]

The five principles of influence we've just discussed work best on heuristic thinkers. They're like mental shortcuts, guiding a teen's thinking or actions with a minimum of mental exertion on his or her part. Thus, when our students utilize one or more of these principles with a friend, they have the best chance of being effective if they know that the friend is in a heuristic-thinking mode. Because as soon as that friend changes modes of thinking, the principles become almost useless.

The opposite of heuristic thinking is *systematic* thinking. Some teenagers are naturally systematic thinkers; others slip back and forth between heuristic and systematic.[4] In fact, what is so interesting and challenging about students in this postmodern generation is that they have the ability to fluctuate between the two. We are ministering to the most technological and information-savvy generation that has ever existed!

If an unbelieving teenager happens to be thinking systematically, the principles of influence are likely to have less of an impact. Students who process thoughts systematically find the loopholes. They sniff out the inconsistencies in our students' lives. To the extent that lost students are thinking systematically in a situation, a principle of influence may not work; using it might even make our students look foolish.

Eventually every teenager will get around to processing a life or a message systematically. It may not happen quickly; but sooner or later, they will ask the hard questions. That's why it's good for us to spend time preparing our students to give an answer for the hope they profess and live for. The key is for our core students to build a relational bridge that will allow them to know when a friend is thinking heuristically (meaning that he or she is open to influence by comparison, reciprocity, or another principle) and when that friend is thinking systematically (meaning a more direct and logical approach is necessary).

Modeling

Let's look at two more concepts that can be helpful to our students when it comes to influencing their peers. The first, *modeling*, is somewhat similar to the principle of comparison. It refers to the dominant means by which all of us acquire new ideas and behaviors: by watching what other people do. Learning through modeling requires very little thinking. All we have to do is copy the model; we don't have to try to figure out everything that is going on and come up with an appropriate behavior.

Think of a typical church service, for example. Most

people in the service know what to do and when to do it; they know what not to do and when not to do it. Anyone who doesn't know the drill sticks out like a sore thumb. It usually doesn't take long for the newcomer to start imitating everyone else's example.

Or think of what happens at summer camp. A student who has been hanging back, observing, sees other teenagers going to the front of the room during worship night after night—lifting their hands, singing with their eyes closed, and dancing (unless they are Baptist; then they're "moving rhythmically") with obvious joy and freedom. By the end of the week, that observer-student has become a participating student, singing and dancing with hands lifted high at the front of the room.

In the best-case scenario, the modeling leads to the desired consequence. The spectator-student observes peers who are full of joy and freedom. He or she wants the same experience. If modeling then leads to that desired experience, it has been effective. If, however, the student does not experience joy and freedom by doing what the other students are doing, he or she will quickly drop the model.

What's on the Runway?

Two factors affect how modeling works in a particular teenager's life. The first is the sheer number of models to choose from. Our students sit in classrooms and walk the halls with peers who have a wide variety of values and belief systems. The choice of which model to follow isn't always a slam-dunk.

The second factor is that different teenagers interpret what is being modeled in different ways. Thirty students may see the same model, but what they learn from that model varies. Let's say the class clown gets thrown out of the science lab and sent to the office for setting fire to a dissected frog. From this model many of the students learn that bad behavior gets punished and ought to be avoided. Other students learn that the best way to get out of a science lab is to act up in class. Others learn that as long as they don't set fire to the frogs, they can get away with almost anything else.

Here's the bottom line: Whenever things happen, people are modeling *something*. Exactly *what* they're modeling, however, is open to interpretation. The ramifications of this are huge. When teenagers focus their eyes on the wrong people, they potentially damage their sensitivity to truth. Sensitivity to truth, just like sensitivity to light, deteriorates gradually, almost imperceptibly. That is why our students can lovingly warn their friends of the perils of the paths they are walking down, and those friends can fail to adhere to their advice or ignore them completely. It is why parents can continually talk to their sons and daughters about poor choices or bad habits, and their children can't see where they are or where they are headed.

Some of our students' friends have seen and focused on the wrong stuff and the wrong people for so long that they have slowly lost their vision. Things are fuzzy. What's clear to those around them is not clear to them. So they desire the wrong things, gravitate toward the wrong people, and live accordingly. When our students try to speak truth to them, they just look at them like, "What are you talking about?" Their eyes have grown accustomed to the darkness. The light of truth seems too harsh, too extreme.

At one point the truth was much more tangible and clear to most teens. Now it's not. No cheating on tests used to be a standard—but students have seen their friends do it over and over again, make good grades, and not get caught. Obeying Mom and Dad used to be important—but they've seen many of their friends rebel against their parents' authority, have a blast every weekend, and never get grounded. Sex before marriage used to be a no-no—but their friends keep doing it, and no one's pregnant (yet). Now sex is no big deal.

Getting Noticed

This is what happens when teenagers fix their eyes on the wrong people. It more than amplifies the reason why our students have to be a visible and viable influence in the lives of their unbelieving friends. But jumping up and down on the lunch table and screaming, "Look at me!" is not the ticket. Nor is responding only when trouble is in the air. No, the thing that will get our students noticed is a consistent, compassionate, and godly life lived out day after day.

Modeling, we're convinced, is the most effective method our students have for influencing the thinking and behavior of their peers. And for many of our students, it just may be the missing piece of the puzzle. Our students want to convince their friends they need Christ. But their best efforts to talk their friends into faith never seem to get them very far. Talk is cheap; what they need is relational leverage. Modeling helps them gain crucial ground. It helps them build relational bridges. Persuasion will have its place and will offer itself in time.

Conditioning

The next concept of influence we need to explore is *conditioning*. This is an extremely common form of influence. If you have a dog and you feed it canned food, what happens every evening when you hit the can opener? The animal comes running, even if you are opening a can of green beans. The dog has associated the sound of the opener with its food and has been conditioned to respond that way.

Conditioning works with people too. Go to K-Mart and watch what happens when the blue light turns on. Cost-conscious shoppers make a beeline to the blue-light table because they associate the light with a good sale. Research has proven that people are more likely to buy the sale item under the blue light, even if the item isn't really a good value.

But you know what conditions people faster than a blue light? Emotions—particularly emotions that are intense and negative. Stuart vividly remembers the trauma he experienced as a child in a Hickory Farms cheese and meat shop in the mall. It was Christmas time, and the store was giving away free samples. Being both young and hungry, Stuart casually walked up to the sample display and reached for a toothpick, intending to stab a piece of sausage and cheese. For reasons only God knows, the lady behind the counter (who, Stuart says, closely resembled the lunch lady passing out sloppy Joes in the movie *Billy Madison*) screamed at him to get out of the store and jabbed his extended hand with a toothpick.

Shocked and frightened, Stuart ran out of the store bawling. To this day he breaks into a cold sweat if he sees a huge beef stick or a cheddar-cheese disk—and he practically hyperventilates whenever he walks by a Hickory Farms store. Many years and numerous counseling sessions have come and gone, but the Hickory Farms logo is still so strongly associated in his mind with that frightening day that the old emotions come roaring back.

Conditioning happens in all kinds of arenas. Our culture has even been conditioned to respond in certain ways to Christianity and the church. The aftermath of the terrorist attacks on September 11 was a conditioned response to the very best of what the church ought to be. People flocked to churches to find solace, peace, and hope. Interestingly, they evacuated the churches almost as quickly as they invaded them. Why? Did the emotion of the horror of those events wear off? We don't think so. Maybe the answer lies in what they found—or didn't find—when they got there.

Don't you want your students to be the ones their lost peers run to when trouble or tragedy strikes? When things get crazy in their lives, these teenagers ought to think of our students first as the people they can confide in, ask advice of, and count on. It should break our hearts that students with no hope run to friends with the same lack of hope, when hope is their greatest need!

Consider the numerous stories in the Gospels of people who, in the direst of situations, sought Jesus out. Why did a Roman officer come looking for Jesus when his servant was dying? Why did lepers and paralytics seek him? Because, in many ways, Jesus had conditioned them to do so. He was always available and helpful, compassionate and accepting. The people saw him like this day after day.

89

Right now our core students are conditioning their unbelieving friends to think of God in a particular way. They are modeling a picture of God. Is it a huge masterpiece, like the ceiling of Michelangelo's Sistine Chapel in Rome, which one cannot pass without stopping and considering? Or is it a fuzzy Polaroid, worth no more than a quick glance and all too easily tossed aside?

The degree to which your students will be influential in the lives of their lost peers hangs upon that answer.

Pressure Points

1. How would you define success as it relates to your students and influence?

2. What steps are you taking to develop students who are exceptional bridge builders to their peers?

3. Read 1 Peter 2:11–12. What does this passage say to you about the influence our students need to gain with lost friends? How do they gain that influence, according to Peter's words?

4. Which of the principles of influence discussed in this chapter seem to operate in your students' lives the most? Which seem to operate the least? Why?

5. How has your youth ministry conditioned students to think and act toward the truth of the gospel?

The Principles

Scientists at NASA built a gun specifically to launch dead chickens at the windshields of airliners, military jets, and space shuttles traveling at maximum velocity. The idea was to simulate the frequent collisions that occur with airborne fowl and test the strength of the vehicles' windshields. When British engineers heard about the gun, they were eager to test it on the windshields of their new high-speed trains. Arrangements were made, and a gun was sent across the Atlantic.

In the first simulation, the British engineers watched in shock as the chicken hurled out of the barrel of the gun, crashed into the supposedly shatterproof windshield, smashed it to smithereens, blasted through the control console, snapped the engineer's backrest in two, and embedded itself in the back wall of the cabin—like an arrow shot from a bow.

The horrified Brits sent NASA the disastrous results of the experiment, along with the designs of the windshield. They begged the U.S. scientists for suggestions.

NASA responded with a one-line memo:

"Defrost the chicken."[1]

The principles that follow are the "frozen chickens" of developing influential students. They are the principles our Christian teenagers need to embrace in order to have influence and leverage with their peers. They're what they need to "break through."

Don't defrost.

If you don't stand for something, you will fall for anything.

AUTHOR UNKNOWN

4

The Standards Principle

Gaining the High Ground

We are often asked, "Why should Christian students have friends who don't have their own relationship with Christ?" Our answer is simple: "Without unbelieving friends, how can our students share their faith and make disciples?"

We understand that youth ministry can be frustrating. Youth leaders often get discouraged by the low student participation in evangelistic outreaches and low baptism counts semester after semester. But the truth is, the low numbers are the result of the paradox in which our students have been inadvertently placed. We press them to win their friends to Christ. We challenge them to bring their lost friends to church (and even scold them in love when they fail to do so). With equal fervor, however, we admonish them to have nothing to do with people who are lost. We encourage them not to have lost friends.

How can they do both? One message cancels out the other.

Reaping the Benefits

We're convinced that having friends who are unbelievers is not a bad thing for Christian students. In fact, there are some specific benefits. Let's look at two.

Spiritual Growth

This may seem counter-intuitive, but unbelieving friends can help our students grow spiritually. In fact, the lid that some of your Christian students seem to have on their personal spiritual growth is probably due to their lack of friendships with lost peers. Part of the apathy you sense stems from the fact that they are not spiritually challenged by peers who think and believe differently than they do. For so long we as youth ministers and parents have encouraged Christian students to run from anyone who doesn't think the same as they (or we) do. But as I heard Bill Walton, former UCLA and NBA basketball great, comment recently on TV, "If everyone is thinking the same, no one is thinking."

Having friends who question their faith is as healthy for our Christian students as it is the students doing the questioning. Responding to queries of who, what, why, and how requires them to dig for answers that go deeper than "because my youth leader said so" or "because I read it in the Bible."

When everyone in a teenager's world thinks, says, and

believes the same thing, spiritual growth is difficult to attain. The dynamics of weightlifting apply here: Muscle growth occurs when resistance is met. You can't build physical muscles without resistance. And you can't build spiritual muscles without the same. Is it any wonder that so many of our students get knocked out when they hit the university campuses, where everything they've believed in is questioned? In high school their faith was never challenged. Their faith muscles were never pressed to grow. Now they're the weaklings at the beach, and the world is kicking sand in their faces.

A challenged faith becomes a strong faith. But that's not the only dynamic at work in producing spiritual growth. On a very practical level, a teenager's efforts at spiritual growth intensify when he or she knows that others are watching. We all perform better when someone is watching, don't we? It's a fact of life. A basketball player's intensity and focus increase when the girl of his dreams walks into the gym and sits in the stands. A teenage daughter works harder on her homework when her dad is looking over her shoulder. And we all jog faster and with better form when cars are coming as opposed to when we're all alone on the road.

Some of the greatest times of spiritual growth our students will ever experience will come when they know they have lost friends who are intently watching their lives. On the other hand, Christian students who don't have unbelieving friends watching them will eventually become spiritually lazy.

Sad to say, but our youth ministries are full of bored Christian teenagers. They are like soldiers who never go to war. Soccer players with no game to play. Some students become so bored with their faith that they start looking around for something new to spark their interest. Often these are the students who get caught up in tangents. They're the ones who strive to become *Purpose Driven Youth* while *Fishing the Planet* as they apply *The Seven Checkpoints* and pray *The Prayer of Jabez for Sixteen Year Olds* while singing songs from the latest Passion CD at See You at the Pole. And what is our typical response to their boredom? More programs. In many of our youth ministries, we use programs like spiritual Ritalin.

Recently, a student walked up to one of our leaders at North Point Community Church and complained that he wanted and needed deeper Bible study. He had been reading the writings of a particular modern theologian and felt we needed to teach at that level. Understand, this is a kid who never misses a youth meeting. He attends a Christian academy that has chapel once per week and Bible classes every day.

His perceptive small group leader asked him, "Are you investing in any friends who don't know Christ?"

"No," the student answered.

"Then the deepest thing you can do at this point in your Christian walk is to invest your time and effort in someone who needs Jesus," the leader challenged him.

That kind of investment is a boredom slayer—and not just for students. Have you ever noticed that denominations, which often disagree vehemently on certain doctrinal points when they have nothing better to do, tend to cooperate with one another on the mission field? The reason is simple: They have a common goal. Minor differences have nothing to do with the mission at hand. There is no time on the mission field to be lazy or bored; too much is at stake. When you are investing in others for the sake of the glory of God, everything in life takes on a whole new significance.

The Right Balance

A second thing unbelieving friends can do for our students is keep them from becoming unbalanced.

When someone says the word *ghetto*, what comes to your mind? Most of us probably think of specific geographical areas with populations of low socioeconomic status. But by definition, a ghetto is simply a subculture. And all subcultures have distinctives that "brand" them—they have their own kinds of music, language, and fashion sense, for example. Anyone who is not indoctrinated and familiar with a specific subculture feels alienated and disconnected within that subculture. They feel out of balance in the midst of it.

Christianity and youth ministry, in particular, have become a ghetto of sorts. Some of our churches and youth ministries are like self-contained neighborhoods with food courts, coffee shops, weight rooms, and athletic club memberships. We have our own language. (When we speak Christian-ese, most normal people have no clue what we're talking about.) We have our own clothing. (You can probably go to your dresser right now and pull out at least one camp T-shirt with a scripture reference on it.) We have our own television shows, radio stations, and bookstores. We have our own music—we even have our own boy bands. And many of our core students have become so indoctrinated into this "youth group" subculture that they are unable to connect relationally with anyone outside of it. They are out of balance in the real world.

Basically, our students have three alternatives:

- They can surround themselves with Christians and eventually become lazy, unbalanced, spiritually bored rabbit chasers.

- They can immerse themselves in the "lost world" lifestyle and let their unsaved peers lead them to destruction.

- They can commit themselves to making an impact in their sphere of influence by developing balanced friendships with non-Christian peers according to God's guidelines.

Let's be very clear: For teenagers there is a razor-thin line between influencing others and being influenced. Non-Christian friends can be devastating to a teenager's spiritual growth. We all know students for whom getting away from their non-Christian friends was the best thing that ever happened to them spiritually.

And the truth is, if Christian teenagers develop friendships with non-Christians but ignore God's guidelines for those friendships, they *will* go down. If they learn to develop balanced friendships according to God's principles, however, they can build effective relational bridges and become influential in their friends' lives.

Setting the Standard

Understanding this tension leads us to the first principle of developing students of influence: In order for our students to be influential without being influenced, they must develop, be able to articulate, and live by personal standards. By *develop* we mean they must learn how to derive and arrive at convictions that become standards in critical areas of their lives. Then they must learn how to articulate those standards simply, clearly, and with confidence. Finally, a standard not applied is no standard at all; it's a convenience, not a conviction. Therefore our students must learn how to live out their standards in the circumstances of their day-to-day lives.

In order to be influential without being influenced, you must develop, be able to articulate, and live by personal standards.

Paul was very strong in his challenge to the church in Ephesus as it relates to standards:

> But among you there must not be even a hint of sexual immorality, or of any kind of impurity, or of greed, because these are improper for God's holy people. . . . Have nothing to do with the fruitless deeds of darkness, but rather expose them. For it is shameful even to mention what the disobedient do in secret. (Ephesians 5:3, 11–12)

The unspoken implication from these verses is that our students must have certain specific standards that distinguish them from their peers. And these standards must be nonnegotiable. Christian students cannot become influential without being influenced if they don't have standards. The space shuttle will literally self-destruct and evaporate into millions of pieces at Max Q if the substance of the vehicle has been the least bit weakened or compromised. Our students will self-destruct, too, if they compromise their standards.

A standard is a rule. It's like a fence for a dog: It keeps him in the yard to play to his heart's content, but it also keeps him out of the street. Of course, a standard restricts freedom in a sense, and nobody likes that. Not even God. In the perfect world of Eden, God gave Adam and Eve 99 percent freedom and only 1 percent rule. Most students don't realize that God prefers freedom to rules. When we try to tell them, they ask, "Well, then, why does a God who loves freedom so much make so many rules to restrict it?"

The answer is clear: In this world there are activities that, once partaken of, restrict freedom. And since God is all for freedom, he doesn't want our students involved in anything that will restrict it. Think of it this way: To be free to smoke is to lose a host of greater freedoms. Ask any man or woman who is dying of lung cancer which freedom they would prefer—the freedom to smoke, or the freedom to live? The freedom to smell good, or the freedom to smell like an ashtray twenty-four hours a day?

For our students to be free to put anything they want into their minds sacrifices their freedom to control their thoughts and perspectives on sex, parents, authority figures, and life in general. To be free to fool around with sex as much as they want sacrifices their freedom to one day enjoy a marriage partner to the maximum. It sacrifices their freedom from guilt and shame.

Who is more free: a teenager with a baby or a teenager

without? A teenager with a drinking problem or a teenager without? A teenager with an education or a teenager without?

Adam and Eve decided to do things their own way for the sake of freedom. But did they gain freedom or lose it? And why? They were unwilling to take God at his word and live under the standard he had set. They thought they would gain freedom by disregarding the standard. Instead they lost freedom—and a whole lot more.

Here's the bottom line: Students who develop and live by standards aren't losing their freedom; they're protecting it. This idea is consistent with the "Ultimate Authority" principle in *The Seven Checkpoints*: Maximum freedom is found under God's authority. We teach students this principle by using the visual of an umbrella. As long as you stay under an umbrella in the midst of a downpour, you are protected from the elements. However, the second you decide to step out from under that protection, you are at risk of danger. In a similar way, the moment a Christian teenager steps out from under the umbrella of the authority of God's Word, he or she is at risk of consequences.

Standards are imperative if our students are going to interact with peers who believe, talk, and live differently than they do. Why? Because God is trying to take away their freedom? No. Because he wants them to be free. And they need to set their standards now, ahead of time. An on-the-spot decision made in a peer-pressured environment is almost always the wrong decision.

Of course, students always want to know exactly how many standards they need to set. What's the least amount they can get away with? Here's the answer we give: The more dangerous the environment, the more rules you need.

The Why Factor

One of the most painful realities we had to face when we began this journey was the fact that our students could be influential and share Christ easily and effectively with strangers on mission trips, but they struggled with their peers in their own high schools. We soon realized why: Our students had "testimony malnutrition" at home. On mission trips our students weren't around long enough for unbelieving teens to evaluate whether or not they were for real. But back at school, their peers saw them every day and knew that their proverbial talk did not always match their actual walk.

The truth is, standards are the thing that will set our students apart in the minds of their unbelieving friends. Standards are the separation factor. And they are the primary tool God will use to get the attention of their unsaved friends. Standards are the catalyst that will cause unbelieving peers to finally ask the question our students have been dying for them to ask: "Why?"

"Why did you leave the party?"

"Why won't you try it?"

"Why are you always so nice to that person?"

And just like a raised hand in class, an unbelieving friend's why gives our students permission to speak truth into his or her life. In our present paradigm of student evangelism, we have conditioned our students to answer questions that, quite frankly, their lost friends aren't asking. To knock on a stranger's door and present an answer to an unasked question is very presumptuous, isn't it? Have you ever been around someone who continuously gives you his or her unsolicited opinion on everything under the sun? What do you do with people like that? I know what I do. I get away from them. They start to irritate me.

As youth leaders it's our job to help our students "always be prepared to give an answer to everyone who asks you to give the reason for the hope that you have" (1 Peter 3:15)—not prepared to answer questions that aren't being asked. But prepared because they've earned the right to be heard; and then, when they're asked to speak, prepared to articulate truth in a clear and simple way that captures the imagination and engages the heart of the questioner.

Answering the why question can be one of the most frightening steps of faith a teenager will ever take. All of us have felt that knot in our stomachs when we realize that the moment is now. Time to put up or shut up. Our students can fade at this point, mainly out of concern for what their friends will think of them. We must help them see that the majority of the people who put them down or ridicule them for their standards once held those same standards but compromised. Who, then, has the right to be critical? What would our students rather be guilty of: consistency or compromise?

Some students have had relationships with lost peers for a very long time, but they have never been asked the why question. There are two possible reasons for this. First, it may be that their friends simply need more time to come around. Or second, our students' standards may be weak—

or nonexistent. Which leads us to a greater question: How do we help our students develop strong and consistent standards?

Wisdom, Knowledge, and Action

We have crystallized the process of developing a standard into an easy-to-remember formula:

Biblical Principle or Command + Wisdom = Standard

To understand this standard formula, let's break down the equation.

Principles and Commands

Most teenagers think the Bible is nothing more than a rule book. And of course, Scripture is full of imperatives, or commands, from God. The Ten Commandments is the most well-known example of things God wants us to do and not do. But the truth is, Scripture has more *principles* than it does *commands*. Principles are cause and effect: If you do this, then that will happen.

One way to understand the difference between commands and principles is to think of road signs. Let's say you're driving home and you see a sign that says Speed Limit 55 MPH. That's a command. It's the law. (Some of us forget to obey it sometimes—but we won't go there.)

Later on that same road, you come to a curve that is marked with several yellow signs with black arrows indicating a sharp left turn. Just preceding the arrow signs is another sign that says Slow Down. Now, there is no law that says you must slow down to a certain speed and curve left. But if you don't slow down and curve left, you may quickly find that you no longer exist. (And if you are on the road to Stuart's house, you will wind up airborne and landing in a pond!) The speed limit sign is a command; the Slow Down and arrow signs are more like principles.

Adding Wisdom

To develop a standard, you must start with a command or principle and add a key ingredient: wisdom. Wisdom itself is a combination of two things: knowledge plus action. As youth leaders we have seen the consequences of teenagers applying one without the other. Some students have all the Bible knowledge in the world, but they never use it in a way that might impact others for Christ. Other students are full of zeal, always ready to run off half-cocked, but they have no idea how to answer the why question when it's asked.

Scripture warns against becoming imbalanced in this regard. James challenges us, "Do not merely listen to the word, and so deceive yourselves. Do what it says" (James 1:22). In other words, knowledge without active obedience is deceptive and foolish. On the other hand, Solomon tells us, "It is not good to have zeal without knowledge, nor to be hasty and miss the way" (Proverbs 19:2). In other words, to act without knowledge is equally foolish.

True biblical wisdom is the melding of knowledge and action together. And we're convinced it's the missing tool in the toolbox of Christian teenage America. Youth ministries across the country send graduating class after graduating class into a world where wisdom is a necessity—and where a lack of wisdom spells four years, if not a lifetime, on the treacherous open seas of relative thought and painful consequences. Yet we tend to program our ministries to answer all of our students' questions for them rather than challenging them to come to the same conclusions themselves. And it's only in that challenge that wisdom is born.

Mike Krzyzewski, head basketball coach at perennial power Duke University, speaks well to this. In his book *Leading from the Heart* (one of our favorite books on leadership), he notes that "many people set rules to keep from making decisions."[1] He believes that if his players never develop the ability to ask questions, if they never learn the art of critical thinking, they will not, in the end, be able to withstand pressure and perform at the highest level possible. He goes so far as to have only one rule for his basketball team: Do not do anything that is detrimental to yourself, because if it is detrimental to you, it will bring dishonor to Duke basketball and Duke University.

Some may say this rule is not specific enough. You could even argue that it goes against the idea of setting standards. On the contrary: Coach K has only one rule so that his players can begin to develop the ability to discern between right and wrong, to ask critical questions, to develop standards on their own, to become wise. His one rule forces his players to always question what they are doing or what they're thinking about doing. It literally sets the course for their future, both on the team and after graduation. And as Coach K says so well, "Whatever a leader does now sets up what he does later. And there is always a later."[2]

The genius of this approach, when applied to youth ministry, is that it gives us as leaders the right and the latitude to lead and direct our students based on their individual levels of spiritual maturity. Coach K states it this way: "Too many rules get in the way of leadership. They just put you in a box and, sooner or later, a rule-happy leader will wind up in a situation where he wants to use some discretion but is forced to go along with the same decree that he has concocted."[3] Let's face it. Even our core students are at different maturity levels spiritually. We need to give ourselves the latitude to help them become spiritually influential at their own level and pace. This does not lower the expectation. The standard is still extremely high, worthy of a student's commitment, and consistent with truth. But we are not boxed in to a one-size-fits-all program for helping them achieve that high standard.

In *The Seven Checkpoints*, we told a story about a kid named Matt. The night before our students were leaving on a mission trip, Matt came to us broken and seeking Christ. He asked if there was any way he could go with us. Now understand, every student participating in the mission trip had gone through several months of fairly rigorous study, training, and practice. Matt had not. But because we had reserved the latitude to lead and because our students understood that, the decision was simple. Matt made the trip. And he will tell you to this day that it was the most pivotal week of his life.

Failing Forward

When it comes to helping students develop wisdom, one of the hardest things for us as youth leaders and parents is balancing our natural desire to protect our teenagers and keep them morally and physically safe versus their need to have the freedom to fail. We don't like it, and we have tried to excise it from our homes and ministries; but the truth is, failure is one of life's greatest teachers.

Think about it. We actually learn very little from our successes. Most of the invaluable lessons of life come from our failures. That's why we read books written by successful people who failed and learned from their mistakes. Experience breeds wisdom. As former New York Mayor Rudy Giuliani writes, "There's no substitute for personal experience when it comes to dealing with problems. That's particularly true in times of crisis, when there's less time to develop ideas and plans. Wisdom gained from one's own history provides a head start."[4]

The standard that is untested is the weakest standard of all. When tested, students may goof. They may mess up. They may fail. Better stated: They *will* fail. The only question is, where? Where would you and the parents of your students desire for them to fail as they test their standards: within the context and influence of your home and ministry, or on some faraway college campus? As parents we can definitively say we want our own children to fail while we still have strong voices in their lives. We want the same thing for the students in our ministries.

Our students' ability to develop and set strong standards depends upon whether or not they are allowed to test those standards—and how they respond when they fail. We are critical players in this process. Our relationship with our teenagers must be of such strength that they feel confident about testing their standards at the risk of failure.

Fiue Areas Where Standards Are a Must

In the *Max Q Student Journal* that accompanies this book, we ask students to spend two entire weeks working through this idea of developing standards. We identify five critical areas in which we believe students must have established standards: dating and sex, friendship, entertainment, drinking, and parties. Certainly we could have named more. But when we considered the day-to-day challenges most students face, we felt these five were particularly crucial. If our goal is to develop students who can be influential without being influenced themselves—who can withstand Max Q and make it through intact—then we must challenge them to ask the hard questions and develop strong standards in these five areas.

Dating and Sex

This is probably the toughest one for teenagers. When the hormones get cranked up, standards for dating and sex tend to get lowered to half-mast. Many Christian students who've lost their testimony with their unbelieving friends have done so in this context.

There are two groups of students in this area: those who have had sex and those who have not. Those who have think it's too late to develop standards. Those who haven't think they don't need standards. Both are wrong.

Just about every student within the scope of your influence and mine will be tempted in the area of sex. And at that moment, having sex may seem like the right thing to do. That's why we must encourage our students to decide right now how far they will go and draw that line.

The higher they set their standard, the less danger they'll be in if, in a moment of insanity, they mess up and lower it. For example, let's say Chip's sex and dating standard is holding hands only, no kissing. But one night in a moment of passion, while watching an Adam Sandler movie, he breaks his rule. What has he done? He has kissed a girl. The consequences will be minimal (unless she has bad breath and a canker sore). But what if Chip's standard is that he will have oral sex but not intercourse, and one night, in a moment of passion, he breaks his rule? What has he done? He has had intercourse, and the consequences are more than significant. They may have lifelong implications.

Students who set high standards in the area of dating and sex not only protect themselves and their testimonies, they also blow their unbelieving friends' minds. If teenagers can resist sex, something *must* be different! They reveal an inner strength that their friends cannot deny or ignore. We encourage our students to challenge themselves with these hard questions:

- How far do you want your next boyfriend or girlfriend to have gone with his or her previous date?

- Which story do you want to tell to the person you marry one day: "I waited for you"; "I blew it at sixteen, but I made up my mind after that to wait for you"; or "I blew it and decided what the heck . . . "? Which story do you want to hear?

- What kind of person should you date? Is dating only people who say they are Christians narrow enough? What are the characteristics you are looking for in a future spouse?

- What are you going to do when your friend wants to fix you up with his or her sibling or best friend? Are you willing to appear snobbish? Are you willing to be misunderstood?

Friendship

In *The Seven Checkpoints,* we make this statement: "Your friendships determine the quality and direction of your life."[5] This is a proven, unarguable fact. Many times friends have a greater influence on our students than anyone else. Clearly, a student's choice of friends is important! But that doesn't mean he or she must avoid all teenagers who don't believe in Christ. How else will those teenagers be reached for Christ? The main thrust of *Max Q* is to help you help your students find that delicate balance between avoiding unhealthy friendships and influencing their lost peers.

We encourage our students to ask some pretty hefty questions as it relates to friendship:

- What does a healthy friendship look like?

- Are *you* becoming a friend worth having?

- Do you have Christian friends who are concerned about

111

your relationship with Christ and equally concerned about their own relationship with Christ?

- Do you have boundaries when it comes to friends who don't have a relationship with Christ?

Entertainment

If our students don't develop standards in the area of entertainment (music, movies, videos, magazines, and so on) they will soon find themselves being entertained by sin. As Christians we send a double message when we laugh at sin and then try to convince other people they need to quit sinning. Students always try to rebut this idea by saying, "But my friends will think I'm too good for them if I say I really don't want to see that movie." What is amazing about this response is that hypocrisy is something teenagers detest more than homework (almost). They don't seem to understand that the alternative to having unbelieving friends think they are too good for them is having unbelieving friends think they are hypocrites.

We encourage our students to ask themselves questions such as:

- Does this CD glorify sin in its lyrics?

- Does this movie use sin to attempt to entertain me?

- What will I not watch or listen to?

- What specific areas in entertainment cause me to struggle?

Drinking

Any conversation about alcohol and teenagers has to start at this point: A student under the legal drinking age who decides to drink is already violating a God-given standard. Romans 13:1 is very clear that Christians are to submit to the governing authorities that God has established. Consequently, to drink while under age is to rebel against authority and, ultimately, against God.

But we also need to be painfully realistic. Many of our students are not adhering to that standard. There are Christian students who drink. And they need to be challenged to critically think through their choice to do so.

As with sex, there are usually two camps when it comes to teenagers and alcohol: those who have partaken and those who have not. Those who have usually think it is too late to develop a standard. Those who haven't usually think they don't need a standard. Both are wrong. Generally speaking, teenagers drink because they have never set standards about where they will and will not go and whom they will and will not go with. They drink—even though they know they shouldn't—because they never decide not to.

Virtually all teenagers who have never tasted alcohol will experience a real temptation to drink at some point. At that moment it may not seem wrong; and if they don't have a standard, they will most likely give in. But as soon as they lift that can or cup to their lips, their ability to positively influence the students around them will begin to dissipate. The fact is, unbelieving friends expect Christian students not to drink.

113

When our students do, their friends lose respect for them—along with all hope that Christ is real and can do something worthwhile in their lives.

Whether our students like it or not, alcohol is a dividing line in teenage America. Choosing not to drink sets them apart immediately. If they have gone out drinking with their friends in the past and then decide to set a no-drinking standard, they can expect a certain amount of rejection. Many of their so-called friends will show their true colors by choosing a liquid in a can over them. But at least our students will have an opportunity to begin rebuilding a consistent testimony.

We encourage our students to sit down at home by themselves and write out the pros and cons of drinking. At the bottom of the two columns, we ask them to answer this question: "Will I be a more effective witness if I drink or if I don't drink?" We challenge them to make a decision about alcohol now, when the pressure is not on—when they aren't in the middle of Max Q.

Parties

If our students are making relational connections with their peers, then their unbelieving friends are going to invite them to parties from time to time. Our students must decide in advance what kinds of parties they will and will not go to. And most importantly, they must be willing and able to leave if the environment turns negative. In fact, if our students don't possess the self-assurance and self-control to leave a party when things get out of hand, they are not mature enough to go to parties in the first place.

If you're not willing to leave . . . you're not mature enough to go.

Again, we encourage and challenge our students to ask themselves hard questions such as:

- Should you go to a party where everyone will be drinking, even if you choose not to drink?

- What about a party with no adult supervision?

- At what point will you leave a party, even if it means looking stupid?

- Could simply being present damage your reputation? If people hear that you were at a particular party, what impact will that have on them?

A Punch to the Gut

We have taught the principle of setting standards to students countless times, and it never fails that the same scene materializes. Many students are writing feverishly, asking questions, and interacting with each other. But one group of core students simply sits and stares. They are nonresponsive and act uninterested. (Sadly, these are usually guys.)

So we conclude by asking them, "Do you have standards? We're not asking if you have preferences. Do you have things you are so convinced of that you refuse to compromise on them—regardless of who is asking, how old they are, how good looking they are, where you are, or who will know?" We then make note of the fact that while we were speaking, many of them didn't write even one thing down. It's not that we're legalistic jerks who demand that kids take notes. Nor do we think our communication skills are so unbelievable that everyone should be writing down everything we say. We ask the question because we know that most of the students in the room have lost friends. And most of them really want to be influential in their friends' lives.

And then we ask them to lean in, listen close, and hear this well:

If you're unwilling to develop standards, then you're not mature enough to have relationships with people who are lost.

Without fail, all the air gets sucked out of the room at that point. Not because the students feel guilty for not taking notes, but because they realize they are living lives with no standards. What makes this point even more profound is the fact that Jesus Christ himself gave us the directive to go and make disciples. But if students are unwilling to develop and live by standards, then they aren't mature enough to have relationships with lost friends. And if they can't have relationships with lost friends, they can't make disciples. It's impossible. Who are they going to influence? The bottom line is that Christian teenagers who refuse to develop standards are ultimately refusing to obey the Great Commission. They have put themselves in a position of disobeying Christ.

Strong words? Yes. But true? You tell me.

The High Ground

Down through the centuries, armies that have gone to war have carried a banner, or "standard." They have rallied around their standard, fought for it, even died for it. Scenes of Denzel Washington in *Glory* or Mel Gibson in *The Patriot* come to mind; in these and similar movies, intense fighting is always the backdrop as the standard is lifted and waved in slow motion. The raising of the standard acts like a summons, calling all those who would rise up and fight to join the battle—sometimes against overwhelming odds.

On one of the walls in our offices is a photograph of the Gettysburg National Military Park in Gettysburg, Pennsylvania. The picture shows Little Round Top, which was the most strategic elevation on that old Civil War battlefield. As any military strategist will tell you, the army that has the high ground has the advantage. If you can control the high ground, you can control the outcome of the battle. Apparently, at a very critical point in the Battle of Gettysburg, both the Union and Confederate armies realized simultaneously that neither army occupied Little Round Top. Regiments from both armies literally raced on foot from opposite sides to the top. The outcome of perhaps the most consequential battle in the Civil War was decided because the Union army beat the Confederate army to the high ground!

We can use that picture and its story as a reminder to our students: Their battle is not just to hold certain beliefs. It is not to maintain their safe positions. The battle is to live lives of conviction that reflect the overwhelming passion God has for them and they have for him—and that reflect his passion and theirs for the lost people around them.

God is looking for teenagers who are willing to hold uncompromisingly to their standards. He is looking for teenagers who are not afraid to raise those standards high.

He is looking for students who are ready and willing to race to the high ground.

Pressure Points

1. Discuss this statement with your leadership team: "Part of the apathy you sense in some of your core students stems from the fact that they are not spiritually challenged by peers who think and believe differently than they do."

2. In your opinion, what are the five most critical standards students must establish to gain influence with their peers?

3. Duke basketball coach Mike Krzyzewski says that many people set rules to keep from having to make decisions. What rules do you apply for students within the context of your ministry? To what purpose?

4. Where would you prefer for your students to fail as they test their standards: within the context and influence of your ministry and their homes, or when they are off at college?

5. Do you agree or disagree with this statement: "If a student is unwilling to develop standards, then that student is not mature enough to have relationships with people who are lost"? Why or why not?

When it comes to the whole subject
of loving others, you must know this:
how you handle your own heart
is how you will handle theirs.

JOHN ELDREDGE

5

The Priorities Principle

Putting Your Own Spiritual Health First

The primary purpose for our students establishing friendships with unbelieving peers must be evangelistic.

We realize this probably sounds insensitive and cold. But think about it. How can we say we truly love someone if we don't share our faith—the most important thing in our lives—with that person? Isn't sharing the love of Christ the ultimate expression of love? God is love! Sharing our faith in him with our friends is love to the highest degree.

What's Your Motive?

Generally speaking, however, students aren't thinking about evangelism when they make friends. Their motivation is usually something else altogether.

Let's Hang Out

For example, they may simply be looking for someone to hang out with. On the surface this may not seem like a bad motive. But the truth is, it can lead our students into dangerous territory. As we've said before, acceptance is a powerful motivator for teenagers. Students think, *He seems cool* or, *She seems all right,* so they do whatever it takes to fit in. And in the process of trying to get the other person to like them, they end up making subtle compromises: laughing at the wrong thing, skipping a class, putting someone else down, going somewhere they shouldn't.

Then, when the opportunity comes to share their faith, they look at their new friend and think, *That person won't listen to me. Look at what I've done. I haven't been really bad, I guess—just not very consistent. If I say something about Jesus now, my friend will wonder what's happened to me.* And at that point, a sad reality sets in: The world just scored on those students. Not vice versa.

Missionary Dating

Sometimes the motivation goes a step further: They want somebody to go out with. Again, to most students, this motive may seem harmless. A guy thinks, *That girl is cute, and she seems interested. Going out with her would be cool.* So he makes his move. He strategically shows up at the right place at the right time (having just raided his dad's lifelong supply of Brut by Faberge). He straightens up and flexes what few muscles he has every time she walks by. The girl, meanwhile, has prepared herself by applying so much lip gloss, she looks like she just pulled her head out of a Kentucky Fried Chicken bucket. Both of them do their very best to get noticed. And if they are lucky, the other person complies.

Eventually some dialogue takes place. (Isn't it amazing how guys and girls can go from barely being able to say hello to incessant flirting?) Finally one of them asks the other one out on a date. Dinner and a movie. Hanging out at the local Shell station or Wal-Mart parking lot. You know. A meaningful date.

At some point in the process, if one of the students is a believer, a question surfaces: *Is this person I'm interested in a Christian?* By this time, however, it's usually too late. Relationship has been initiated. The foundation has been laid and set. To change the rules now could mean forfeiting the game altogether.

Too bad they didn't ask the question up front. We tell our students all the time, "If you don't feel comfortable asking, 'Are you a Christian?' or, 'Where do you go to church?' then you're not ready to date. You're not mature enough. If you aren't comfortable discussing spiritual things—supposedly the most valuable and important things in life—*before* a date, then you aren't very likely to discuss them *on* a date. It's almost a guarantee."

Of course, they could ask, "Are you a Christian?" and the other person could say, "Sure!" But is he or she really a believer? We challenge our students not only to ask, but to watch. How does the person act? Talk? What kinds of friends does he or she hang around with—and where? What do other people say about this person? We're not advocating Christian stalking, but it's important to have a good gauge. If students can't tell that someone is a Christian from watching, chances are the person is not a believer—or at least not a strong one.

We especially challenge our girls to be bold. A Christian girl should always find out where a guy stands spiritually before she agrees to go out with him. He wasn't obligated to ask her out; she shouldn't feel obligated to go out with him just because he asked. It's mind-boggling how many of our young ladies go out on dates simply because a guy asked! As for our guys, we encourage them to use church or youth group or some other church-related function as a first date. That way they can set the tone for the relationship and let their date know up front what is important to them without having to preach or beat a drum.

Our students need to understand: The stakes are too high for them to be dating the wrong people. There's no question that God commands Christians not to marry unbelievers. We developed this thought in the previous chapter: Students will probably fall in love with someone they date, and they will probably marry someone they fall in love with. So why play with fire? Christians who date unbelievers are setting themselves up for heartache and complications down the road. A particular relationship may seem harmless at first. But an initial attraction can become an emotional attachment that has the power to sideline wisdom and disconnect a Christian student from God.

A Hard Habit to Break

Dating unbelievers—just like smoking, chewing tobacco, or eating unhealthy foods—can become a bad habit. Just ask Lorie, one of our former students. Despite her love for Christ and passion to see her friends come to know him personally, Lorie battled a horrible habit of dating guys she had no business dating all through high school and college. We're not talking about a ton of guys—just a few who should have been avoided. By the grace of God, Lorie always realized that these relationships were going nowhere fast and broke them off, but always with painful consequences.

Now a college graduate and young professional, Lorie recently had the same thing happen again: another unbeliever, another breakup. Over a cup of coffee in Dallas, she told us the emotional story. She is so angry with herself for winding up in the same old place! She loves God. She loves people. But she'll tell you, dating unbelievers is a hard habit to break. And she has the emotional and spiritual scars to prove it.

How can we help our students avoid the pain and spiritual shipwreck of bad relationships? By reminding them to do what we said in the beginning of this chapter: Keep evangelism as the ultimate purpose for all their friendships with unbelievers. Which leads us to the second principle for developing students of influence: establishing priorities.

The Mask

If you've ever frequented the friendly skies, you've heard the canned flight-attendant spiel—you know, the one that goes, "In case of cabin depressurization, oxygen masks will drop from the overhead compartment . . ." Adult passengers are instructed that, in case of an emergency, they are to place oxygen masks over their own mouths first before helping their children put on their masks.

Doesn't that sound cruel? As parents, our first instinct is to get those oxygen masks on our kids before taking care of ourselves. But if we do that, we're making a mistake. If we pass out from oxygen deprivation, how will we be of any help to our sons and daughters? We can't serve our kids if we are unable to function. Regardless of our deep love for our kids, despite our parental instinct to put them first, the wisest thing to do in an emergency at 30,000 feet is to make our own physical welfare the priority over theirs. Counterintuitive? Yes. But so true.

If we are going to develop students who can be influential without being influenced—who can endure maximum dynamic pressure and still lead others to Christ—we must teach them to do the same thing on a spiritual level: put their own spiritual welfare before the spiritual welfare of others. Mark it down. A time will come when our students find themselves being drawn into things they have no business getting involved in. They will find their motivation shifting from evangelism to acceptance or romance. When that happens, they will need to make their own spiritual growth a priority over the spiritual growth of their lost peers. They will need to decide to back off or perhaps even bail out. Doing so will take courage. And their intimacy with their Creator will depend on it.

Jesus himself applied this principle. He put his own spiritual welfare ahead of the spiritual welfare of others. Consider the feeding of the five thousand (more like twelve thousand when you add women and children) described in John chapter 6. The Bible tells us that "after the people saw the miraculous sign that Jesus did, they began to say, 'Surely this is the Prophet who is to come into the world.' Jesus, knowing that they intended to come and make him king by force, withdrew again to a mountain by himself" (John 6:14–15).

Imagine: Jesus had a huge crowd eating out of the palm of his hand. They would have done anything he said—especially after seeing him turn two sardines and five loaves of Roman Meal nine-grain into a seafood buffet at Red Lobster. They were ready to follow him anywhere. But what did Jesus do? He sensed it was time for him to pray, and he withdrew to a mountain to do so.

When our students find themselves tempted to lower their standards or sacrifice their walk with God in order to stay in a relationship with an unbelieving friend, they need to make their own spiritual health the priority. Their situation is like being in a depressurized plane. They need to reach up, grab God's oxygen mask, and breathe deeply. They can't help their peers if they're not spiritually strong themselves.

Common Excuses

Like parents putting on their oxygen masks first, the idea of backing off or out of a relationship seems counterintuitive to teenagers. This is, after all, the generation that believes in "keeping it real." Translated, our students pride themselves on their loyalty in friendships. Their tendency is to justify their friendships and make excuses for why they can't back out.

There's No One Else

One common justification comes in the form of a question: "If I back out, who is going to reach them? I'm their only Christian friend." But our students must not compromise on this basis.

For one thing, if God was big enough to bring *them* into their friend's life, he is big enough to bring other Christians too. For another thing, Jesus is our example, and he never dropped his standards to please others—even though he was the only savior for the whole world. Jesus refused to compromise in order to reach any of us. Neither should our students compromise to win an unbelieving friend. They must not sacrifice their long-term potential for a short-term relationship.

Snobs R Us

Here's another excuse we hear all the time: "But they won't understand. They'll think I'm a snob!" As we've said before, perception is the cruelest form of reality. Unbelieving peers may think a Christian student who backs away from them is a snob, but *they will be wrong*. On the other hand, if a Christian student keeps compromising in order to hang out with unbelieving friends, those friends will think the Christian student is a hypocrite—and this time they will be right.

So Close

Here's yet another excuse teenagers give for not backing off or bailing out of a relationship: "But my friend is so close to accepting Jesus!" Our students see how far their friend has come in spiritual matters and argue that he or she has come too far for them to back off now. Unfortunately, this comment is usually made by those students who think way too much of themselves and their role in the evangelism process. Who gets the credit for distance traveled—for how close a friend is to a saving relationship with Christ—our students or God?

God knows how close our students' unbelieving friends are to him. He knows much better than they do. And he can do exactly what is necessary to continue the process. Our students need to do what is best for their own spiritual welfare. Consider this: When Jesus fed those twelve thousand people, that was as close as some of them ever got to faith in him— and Jesus still walked away.

Best of Friends

"But he or she is my best friend!" some students object. Well, then, what's best for that friend? Certainly not for our students to compromise, grow spiritually weak, and fail to be a positive influence.

The truth is, as Christians we have not been called to make friends; we have been called to make disciples. Now before you get cynical about that statement, please understand: We can be friends with people and disciple them at the same time. In fact, the whole thrust of this book is that discipling friends is a must. God is not antifriendship. He's the inspiration for the classic "Friends Are Friends Forever"! But our students' eternal purpose must always take priority over temporary relationships— even "best" relationships. When students are no longer following Christ, they can't lead others—not even their best friends— to him.

Smearing the Picture

There is only one thing worse for our students' lost friends than having no Christian friends at all: having compromising Christian friends. The Bible calls compromisers "enemies of the cross" (Philippians 3:18). They give their unbelieving friends a tainted perspective on who God is and what he is like. They paint an inaccurate portrait of God. And before long, in their lost friends' minds, the numbers stop adding up. The reception gets fuzzy. Eventually the connection is lost.

That is why people like Jim Bakker and Jimmy Swaggart have done so much harm to the cause of Christ. Are they forgiven? Absolutely. But forgiveness never negates consequences. We all deal with the residual effect of these and other tainted pictures every day. As youth leaders we see and hear the stories at an all-too-alarming rate: Another youth leader caught in sin. A seemingly solid family divorcing because Dad was not faithful to Mom.

Our students have stories too: A Christian guy begins to date a non-Christian girl, and they become sexually active. In the midst of the relationship, he tries to witness to her. The deeper the relationship grows, the more the young man realizes his sin. He finally reaches the point where he can't take the guilt and shame anymore, and he breaks it off with her. And the girl? She is devastated. She feels used by a guy who claims to know Christ—and she equates Jesus with him.

Bailing out of a friendship for spiritual reasons—before compromise occurs—demonstrates to unbelieving friends just how serious a student's faith is and how real Christ is. It amplifies the priority and the value of that student's relationship with Christ. To do anything less than back off or bail out is to say, "This relationship with my friend is more important to me than my relationship with Jesus."

When the Oxygen Masks Fall

How does a student know when it's time to back off or bail out of a relationship with an unbelieving friend? In an airline emergency, the timing is obvious: the oxygen masks drop out of the overhead compartment. In a relationship emergency, there are obvious cues as well.

Change in Motivation

The first cue is when our students' motivation for pursuing a particular relationship changes. Our students must keep a constant finger on the pulse of their motivation. They must continuously ask why. And when they see that a relationship that started out as evangelistic in purpose has begun to be more about hanging out or romance, then they know they need to back off or bail out.

We see this all the time in youth ministry: a solid Christian girl befriends a guy at school. There are no romantic intentions; she simply wants to see him come to know Jesus. But the more time they spend together, the closer they get to each other, and the more the motivation begins to shade to romance. What happens if she doesn't back off or bail out at this point? She winds up dating and becoming emotionally attached to an unbeliever—someone she set out to win to Christ.

Temptation Island

Another cue for our students is when the temptation to compromise their standards becomes a real battle. Of course, there is a difference between being offered something and being tempted with something. Let's say two Christian students are offered a beer. One student may not be tempted to drink at all, while the other student may find the temptation almost irresistible. Some students are mature enough not to be influenced by certain unbelieving friends, while other students are more easily swayed.

As youth leaders we need to encourage our students to know themselves—to know what tempts them. Then we must encourage them to stay away from those people and environments where temptation is likely to run high. Of course, simply being in a relationship with a lost friend will present points of tension and temptation. Our directive to our students must be: "Whatever you do, make very certain you aren't setting yourself up for a fall." God doesn't lead our students into temptation. That's Satan's job!

Two Strikes and You're Out

Here's another cue: If students violate one of their standards twice, then they need to back off or bail out of the relationship. Why twice? Because the first time our students violate a standard, they need to go to that friend and apologize for compromising. If they apologize, the friend will take notice, and chances are they will never violate that standard again.

And there's another reason. We stated it in a previous chapter: Failure is our greatest teacher. The question isn't, "Will our students fail?" The question is, "Do we want our students to fail within the context of our influence or away from it?" By allowing students to fail at least once, we create an environment of guarded failure.

We admit that we struggled with this idea at first. Our

propensity as youth leaders is to want to protect our students from even one failure. Throughout our journey to develop a ministry of influence, we had to keep reminding ourselves of the kind of students we wanted to develop: students of influence. When we ran the "two strikes" idea through this grid, we realized that we were actually strengthening our students by allowing them to fail. To inoculate them against all failure was to cripple their conviction-building process.

But two strikes, and that's it. Students shouldn't take chances when it comes to their spiritual health. We must encourage them to step away from the batter's box rather than risk striking out. They need to understand: It's never OK to sacrifice their relationship with God for a relationship with a lost friend.

Meet the Parents

The next cue is probably the most neglected one: It's time to back off or bail out when a student's parents say, "It's over!" The truth is, parents have a unique and uncanny insight into their teenagers *and* their teenagers' friends. Parents know when friends are making subtle inroads into their kids' lives. Moms, especially, have an intuition that is almost eerie at times. (We can think of numerous times when our own moms—or our wives—have almost prophetically "called the ball" on something we didn't see.)

In *The Seven Checkpoints*, we state that maximum freedom is always found under God's authority. Our students must learn to submit to the authorities that God has placed over them—and parents are at the top of the list. Disobedience to parents is ultimately disobedience to God. If parents say no to a relationship with a particular friend, students must respect their insight and authority. When Mom and Dad say no, it means no!

Now let's back up a few paces. We know that many parents are skittish about their teenagers having lost friends. So one thing we encourage our students to do is to make a deal with their parents: "If you see this beginning to happen, Mom, just tell me, and I'll back off." We encourage them to tell their parents what they are trying to accomplish with their unbelieving friends. Even better is for students and their parents to put their heads together to establish guidelines for their relationships. Parents and students working together are an amazingly influential team.

The Majestic Whisper

One of the greatest dividends of a relationship with Christ is the privilege of having the Holy Spirit reside within us. The Bible tells us that the Spirit of God sees and discerns all things. He serves as our counselor. He exists to minister to us and to prompt us when we need prompting—to nudge us when we need to move in a particular direction in order to be in the center of God's will.

When the Holy Spirit prompts our students to back out of a relationship with an unbelieving friend, then it's definitely time for them to back out. When they feel a certain inner hesitancy about a relationship, they must be mature enough to recognize the source of that hesitancy, admit that it exists, and back off.

This is why the Spiritual Disciplines principle that we discussed in *The Seven Checkpoints* is so important. Our students need to be able to hear God when he whispers to them. If they don't spend time with God, they won't have ears to hear. They will render themselves deaf to the Spirit's still, small voice.

The Holy Spirit can and will speak to our students. But his wisdom and counsel will do them no good if they can't hear him.

Listening Close

When Katie told us that she was pledging a sorority at Louisiana State University (one of the top-rated party schools in America), we can honestly say we didn't worry about her. It was not that Katie was perfect. It was not that she was incapable of failing. It was that Katie had an inner strength welded by God that is found in few teens. She rushed, joined a sorority, and began to have the kind of influence we pray for all our students to have. Her standards were definitely tested, but they were proved strong. Over her freshman and sophomore years, she personally invested herself in the lives of her sorority sisters and became the most influential girl in her sorority. Her sorority sisters awarded her the highest award any member can receive.

Imagine our surprise, then, when she told us at the beginning of her junior year that she had decided to quit her sorority. Such a thing is almost unheard of in the collegiate Greek system. You don't quit your sorority—especially in your third year! When we asked her why she was quitting, Katie's answer was simple: "God told me to." She'd heard the Holy

Spirit whisper to her. His voice was small and still but obvious: "Quit." So she did.

You might assume that Katie's decision caused her to lose all the influence she had worked so hard to develop with her sorority sisters. Her time there had been wasted. Two years and nothing to show for it. Right? On the contrary, Katie actually gained leverage. Her friends didn't see her as being judgmental. They respected her decision. In fact, her decision only reinforced what she had claimed all along: She belonged to God, and her relationship with him was more important than any other. She still talks with the girls. Many come to her and ask her for advice about life. She has been a bridesmaid in several sorority sisters' weddings. And when Katie got married, many of her sorority sisters were in attendance.

Our students must be in such intimate communion with God that they can hear the Holy Spirit's "majestic whisper."[1] And he will whisper to them for different reasons. It seems clear that God wanted Katie to bail out, not because she was in spiritual danger, but in order to increase her leverage—to actually maximize her influence.

Not Me

Sometimes the Holy Spirit whispers, "Back off," because God is ready to use somebody else to bring a lost person the next step closer to him. There is much biblical precedent for this. Joshua took God's people into the Promised Land—a land that Moses prepared the people of Israel to inhabit but never personally stepped foot in. Solomon built the temple—a temple that David planned for but never personally worshiped in. John the Baptist prepared the way for Jesus and thus served his purpose. The point is obvious: Sometimes God chooses to start a mission with one person and complete it with someone else.

Of course, we all want to see the payoff on our investments, and our students are no different. But sometimes the "majestic whisper" comes because God has prepared someone else to take the lost person the next step. And sometimes God simply wants to encourage another student by giving him or her the joyful experience of leading someone to Christ. The fact is, God is constantly weaving our students' lives and the lives of their unbelieving friends into a great tapestry of interconnecting relationships. Our teens must learn to rest in the truth that "neither he who plants nor he who waters is anything, but only God, who makes things grow" (1 Corinthians 3:7). God may use one student to plant a seed, another student to water it, and somebody else altogether to reap the harvest. In a lost person's journey to faith, each person at each step is important and necessary.

On the Verge

Sometimes the Holy Spirit whispers to our students because he is trying to protect them from getting hurt. Only God knows when they're on the verge of becoming romantic with the person they are trying to influence. Only God knows when they are on the verge of allowing acceptance to become the overwhelming desire that drives the relationship. Only the all-knowing God is big enough to have so vast a perspective. And he cares so much for each of our students! They need to realize that when he whispers for them to back off or bail out, it may be because he sees something dangerous coming their way that they can't see.

Our students need to understand this about the Holy Spirit: He's not someone to argue with. Entering into a debate with God is like trying to outjump Vince Carter or outsing Celine Deon. It's a no-win situation. Of course, God wants our students to engage in meaningful conversation with him. He longs to hear their hearts, and he wants them to hear his heart. He is not afraid to embrace disagreement from his children; that's a natural part of relationship. But in the end, our students must remember that they are arguing with God. Omniscient. Omnipresent. Omnipotent. *That* God. And continually battling with God just isn't wise. Simply stated, God is always right.

There's another reason that it's foolish to argue with God: He could choose to not speak at all. If a student's heart is continually unreceptive to his counsel, God may decide to withhold his voice altogether. What a scary thought—our students, by their own "know-it-all-ism," could cause Creator God to be silent. May it not be so! As youth leaders we need to emphasize to our students that the Holy Spirit is a gift and a God worth listening to and heeding.

The Wrong Exit

For most of our teenagers, the time will come when they realize they need to back off or bail out of a particular relationship. The question is, how do they do it? In the long-term process of influencing lost teenagers for Christ, how our students exit a relationship is as important as how they enter it.

Here Comes the Judge

Unfortunately, the widening gap between Christian teenagers and their lost peers has greatly increased the potential for our students to be judgmental toward their friends. If you have any doubts about this, sit down one day with your students and ask them what their lost peers do wrong. We guarantee you'll get an earful. Christian students can be unbelievable inspectors of specks when it comes to their unbelieving friends. But pointing a white-gloved finger is no way to exit a relationship.

For one thing, judging an unbelieving friend is literally taking a position that Jesus did not take. Remember the story of Jesus and the woman caught in adultery? Jesus didn't pass judgment; instead, he invited anyone who was without sin to cast the first stone. Our students need to understand that backing off or bailing out of a friendship is not an act of judgment. It's an act of wisdom—one that, quite often, has less to do with the problems of the lost friend than with the weaknesses or nonexistent standards of the Christian student.

Judging an unbelieving friend is not only wrong, it's counterproductive. Backing off or bailing out is part of the process of influence. When our students back off, they aren't withdrawing influence; they are setting up and preparing for someone else to continue God's pursuit of their friend. If they exit the relationship with a judgmental attitude, they erect barriers that will only complicate things for the next believer who comes into that person's life.

The Great Houdini

Our students must not judge. Neither should they disappear. We have all seen this happen: A Christian student invests in an unbelieving friend for an extended period of time. Then at some point he or she sees the need to back off or bail out. So what happens? Without any explanation, the Christian student disappears. He or she stops returning phone calls and hides from the unbelieving friend at school.

This kind of "disappearing act" completely distorts the love of God that the student had previously worked so hard to exhibit. The lost friend can't help but feel judged and think, *What's wrong with me?* Yet, as we've said, the problem often has very little to do with the unbelieving friend and everything to do with the Christian student. We must encourage our students not to make excuses. They must be truthful—or risk losing all the ground they gained for Christ in their friend's life.

The Right Way to Get Out

We have created a memorable statement to help students back off or bail out the right way:

> **Say what is true . . . pray before you do . . . and follow through.**

Let's look at each of the components of this statement separately.

Say What Is True

Conjuring up a crazy story that is not remotely close to the truth is hazardous to the process of influence. Telling something that is close to the truth (but not quite) is just as deceptive and dangerous. Our students need to tell their unbelieving friends exactly why they are backing off or bailing out. They don't have to go into a long discourse. It can be something as simple as this: "The most important relationship in my life is the one I have with Jesus Christ. Because I don't want to jeopardize that relationship, our relationship isn't the wisest thing for me to be involved in right now. I need to make God my priority so he can do what he wants to do in me." Honesty is not the best policy; it's the *only* policy.

Pray before You Do

It is imperative that our students seek God and his wisdom through prayer before getting into a conversation with a friend about backing off. Many times God will give them wisdom into their friend's situation—divine insight that they would never have gained any other way. Other times God will give them sensitivity to the right timing, perhaps even arranging a "divine moment" when they can share more than they originally planned. Still other times God will work out the circumstances so that our students barely have to open their mouths. He may move in such a way that the unbelieving friend is the one who backs off.

We need to explain to our students that praying before speaking is an act of submission. God knows what is going to happen. He sees the end. Our students' communion with him in prayer is simply their way of acknowledging his sovereignty in their lives. It releases the control of their situation to God. And it puts the outcome squarely in his hands.

Make Sure You Follow Through

If I told you that I believed that, for the sake of the health and welfare of my family, I needed to stop traveling and speaking, yet I continued to travel and speak, what would you think of my belief system? What would you think of my priorities? You would not have a high regard for what I believe. And you'd laugh in my face if I said, "My family is my top priority."

The same thing holds true for Christian students who claim, "God is my priority, and I need to back off of this relationship," yet they never seem to follow through. Our students can't go back on their word. And by the way, a girl doesn't need to go out to dinner with that guy she has been investing in to talk about it. A guy doesn't need to go to a party with the group of friends he has been investing in to give his explanation. The more intimate the environment, the harder it is to follow through. As the Nike ad says, just do it.

Keeping Your Footing

It's a safe bet that you have students who need to abandon certain relationships and start all over with new ones. Some of your students need *new* unbelieving friends. They have ruined their testimony with the friends they have now. They need to step back and let someone else step in. Some of your students need to quit flirting with those friends whose faith they are not sure about. And all our students need to be reminded: If they're not willing to back off or bail out, then they're not ready to have relationships with unbelieving friends. They will wind up being the ones influenced and pulled down into the lost world's pool of heartache, disobedience, and guilt.

Stuart tells this story from his college basketball days:

My sophomore year was special. Our team finished with a 31–3 record and won the conference championship. We ranked second in total team defense and twelfth overall in the country. What made this achievement even more incredible was that the basketball program was only in its second year of existence. It was the most fun I have ever had playing sports.

To celebrate our remarkable season, our school threw a campus-wide party. By the end of the night, our team wound up at the campus pool; and being the mature people we were, some of the guys started throwing others who didn't want to swim into the deep end. One of the first guys they threw in was Marty, one of our senior players. There was one major problem: Marty didn't know how to swim.

I was talking with a group of people poolside when I heard Marty hit the water and come up screaming and thrashing. It was immediately clear that this was not a good situation. Several of my teammates jumped in the deep end to try to help their drowning friend. Marty was both frantic and pretty strong (for a point guard); and as each teammate tried to help him, they wound up being the ones pulled under. Marty literally tried to crawl on top of each teammate who tried to rescue him.

Teammate after teammate dove in to help, and each one had to literally fight for their lives to keep Marty from drowning them.

Taking in the whole situation, I dove in and swam as fast I could to the shallow end of the pool. I walked out along the slippery bottom into deeper and deeper water, making sure that my footing was secure the whole way. When the water reached my chin, I reached out as far as I could and called out, "Marty, give me your hand!"

Somehow in the midst of the chaos, with teammates bobbing and choking, people yelling instructions, and girls crying, Marty heard me. He thrashed toward me and grabbed my hand. I quickly pulled him to safety. Crying, spitting up water, and still scared to death, Marty just kept repeating, "Thank you! Thank you!"

What happened to Stuart that night is a perfect picture of what has to happen with our Christian students and their lost and drowning peers. Sometimes the wisest thing they can do for the sake of their unbelieving friends is to make their own spiritual health a priority over the spiritual health of the ones they are trying to save. For a student to try to live the Christ-life before an unbelieving friend, when that friend is the one doing the influencing (and not the other way around), is as dangerous as trying to tread water in the deep end with some-one who's drowning.

Our students must keep their feet on solid ground. To do so will seem counterintuitive at times. It will feel wrong. But it is right. In his book *Seizing Your Divine Moment*, Erwin Raphael McManus says, "It is always right to do what's right, even if it turns out wrong. There are times that God calls us to do the right thing, knowing that others will respond in the wrong way."[2]

In fact, sometimes it will be the very thing that brings life to a friend who so desperately needs it.

Pressure Points

1. We stated that if a student does not feel comfortable asking, "Are you a Christian?" or "Where do you go to church?" then that student is not ready to date. He or she is not mature enough. Do you agree or disagree with this statement? Why?

2. What Scripture verses or biblical examples can you think of that reinforce the principle that our students must put their own spiritual welfare before the spiritual welfare of others?

3. Process your thoughts concerning this idea: If students violate one of their standards twice, then they need to back off or bail out of the relationship.

4. Erwin Raphael McManus says, "It is always right to do what's right, even if it turns out wrong. There are times that God calls us to do the right thing, knowing that others will respond in the wrong way." What does this statement have to do with a student's friendships with lost peers?

5. Think of the core students in your ministry. Are certain ones being pulled down by relationships with lost friends? What can you do to help them back off or bail out?

**My best friend is the one
who brings out the best in me.**

HENRY FORD

6

The Accountability Principle

Making Sure Someone Has Your Back

Take a good look at these seven words from John 4:4: "Now he [Jesus] had to go through Samaria."

What do these seven words have to do with developing students of influence? What do they have to do with the topic of this chapter, maintaining accountability? And how does an account of Jesus going through Samaria have anything remotely to do with a rock group from San Diego?

We'll eventually answer all these questions. But first we need to understand: Jesus did not have to go through Samaria for geographical reasons. In fact, because of the intense racial tension between Jews and Samaritans in that day—worse than in the Deep South of the 1960s with its segregated buses, water fountains, and bathrooms—there was a well-beaten path *around* Samaria. Jews would literally travel hundreds of miles out of their way to avoid contact with even one Samaritan.

No, Jesus had to go through Samaria for relational reasons. There were people there who needed life. One Samaritan lady in particular had been coming to a well day after day, but she couldn't get her thirst quenched. Numerous tumultuous affairs had done nothing to meet her deep need. So the Son of God decided to purposely place himself in the epicenter of a volatile environment for the sake of relationship.

What a reflection of the heart of God! Holy, unique, morally perfect Jesus—so passionate about his Father's glory that he would take a road less traveled to offer life to a woman who kept getting it all wrong!

As youth leaders we want to develop students who have that same desire. Students who are willing to go wherever there are people who need to be connected relationally to God. Students who know how to use the living water that flows from them to quench the seemingly insatiable thirst inside the lost teenagers of their generation. Students who can intentionally invest in their peers in a dark environment without compromising their standards or confusing their priorities.

A couple of years ago, *CCM* magazine ran an awesome interview with the members of the rock group P.O.D. (The acronym stands for "Payable on Death.") This foursome from San Diego, California, has taken the rock-and-roll and MTV world by storm, garnering nominations for both Grammy and MTV video awards. They've also been extremely vocal, both personally and musically, about their relationship with Jesus Christ.

Asked about the band's perspective on faith and their calling to reach people with the gospel, Sonny, the lead singer, said this:

> I believe there is a forefront, and on this side is the king-dom of heaven, and on that side is the lost, dying world. P.O.D. has always been folded over on this fence. There are people right up front with us, embrac-ing us, holding onto our legs, strapping us down. On the other side, our hands are going as far as they can, trying to pull the lost into the kingdom of heaven. When you're standing way back on the outskirts, of course you are going to have concerns, because you are looking from a distance. You're wondering, "What's going on over there? Half-way in, half-way out!" But praise God! God has surrounded us with what we need. Kids come out, and they are like, "Dude, I get it."[1]

Did you see it? The visual imagery is powerful: To be influ-ential without being influenced, our students need fellow believers who will hold on to their ankles as they reach out over the fence to their lost peers. That's a picture of accounta-bility. Clearly, God wants our students leaning into the dark and pulling their friends to safety. But without effective accountability, the likelihood that they will fall over the fence is pretty substantial. They must have someone—or many someones—who will strap them down. They must have accountability relationships with mature Christian friends who will ask them the hard questions. Friends who will not let them drift away. Friends who will make sure they keep their relationship with Christ the priority.

This is not an option—it's a must! For students who want to be influential, the principle of accountability is nonnegotiable.

Accountability Defined

Of course, *accountability* has been a Christian buzzword for some time. The Promise Keepers movement elevated it to new heights, as men came out of giant stadiums and immediately formed accountability groups with other men in their churches. But like many things in postmodern Christianity, the word itself has gradually become diluted and misused to such a degree that few students today understand its meaning or purpose. Many teenagers think it's a joke. I mean, how many student accountability relationships do *you* see that are functioning the way they need to function?

In our experience student accountability groups tend to quickly degenerate into glorified "Sinners Anonymous" meetings that go something like this: "Hi, my name is Larry, and I struggle with lust." Everyone replies, "Hi, Larry! We lust too." Then they all pray, "God, help us not to struggle with lust," and move on. Or, "Hi, my name is Sarah, and my issue is jealousy." Everyone replies, "Hi, Sarah! We struggle with jealousy too." Then they pray, "God, help us not to struggle with jealousy," and move on. Or the group leader reads a list of potential sins, and as each sin is named, those who are guilty for that week raise their hands. Then it's on to the next sin. No one takes responsibility for anyone else; they just admit they're all in the same boat.

That is *not* functional accountability!

Here's how we define accountability for our students:

Accountability means giving an individual or group permission to question you in one or more aspects of your life and committing yourself to total honesty with that individual or group.

Permission is a key word. Accountability is a two-way street. If students try to hold one another accountable in areas in which they have not been given permission to ask questions, they won't succeed.

Nor will they succeed if they only talk in generalities. Students need to get specific about the aspects of life they desire accountability in. What specific area of temptation does a student struggle with? Late-night movies? Certain types of music by certain artists? Thoughts about a certain person of the opposite sex? Perhaps a student needs accountability in the area of spending consistent time alone with God. Or Scripture memorization. We know of an accountability group of guys that gives a free arm slug if one of their group members can't quote the Bible verse for the week.

Perhaps a student needs accountability in the area of submission to authority. He or she read *The Seven Checkpoints Student Journal* and knows (in theory) that maximum freedom is found under God's authority; yet rebellion against Mom and Dad is a frequent struggle. Or perhaps accountability is needed in a particular "trouble spot" in a relationship with an unbelieving friend. Whatever the case, the more specific students are about their need, the better they can be held accountable to a godly standard.

151

In effective accountability relationships, students should be able to share anything—their biggest temptations, their deepest hurts, their greatest frustrations. To do so, however, requires a commitment on their part to total honesty. They have to be real about who they are and what they're going through. An accountability relationship built on lies eventually dies. Accountability and dishonesty simply cannot coexist.

No Privacy

Invariably students ask why they need these kinds of relationships. They tend to think their relationship with God is between them and God—and no one else. But nothing could be further from the truth. Our students must understand that their relationship with God is personal, but it is not intended to be private. There's a big difference.

A relationship with God is personal . . . but it's not private.

The confusion is understandable. After all, Christianity is distinguished from other religions in that it is personal. Through Christ we have a personal relationship with the Creator of the universe. The Spirit of God resides personally in our hearts. No other belief system makes even remotely similar claims.

But at no point does the intimacy of our walk with God relieve us from personal accountability to the body of Christ. Your relationship with God is not just your business, and my relationship with God is not just mine. We are accountable to one another. Why do we say that? For three reasons:

Jesus commands us to practice accountability.

Jesus himself considered accountability so important that he commanded his disciples to hold one another accountable. He told his closest followers: "So watch yourselves. If your brother sins, rebuke him, and if he repents, forgive him. If he sins against you seven times in a day, and seven times comes back to you and says, 'I repent,' forgive him" (Luke 17:3–4).

Teenagers don't like this idea of being confronted by other Christians. Neither did the disciples. How do we know? Look at their response: "The apostles said to the Lord, 'Increase our faith!'" (Luke 17:5).

You get the sense from this verse that the disciples looked wide-eyed at Jesus and said, "Dude, I can't do that! You are going to have to amp up the faith quotient in me, because I am not about to take instruction or get rebuked by these guys. I'll take it from you, Jesus—but these bozos? No way!"

But Jesus was making a point: We are in one another's lives for this very purpose. Accountability is our responsibility.

The functioning of the body of Christ necessitates accountability.

The concept of the connectivity of the body of Christ is foreign to many of our Christian students. Yet Scripture plainly tells us that we are all individual parts of one body. Paul elaborates this way:

> The body is a unit, though it is made up of many parts; and though all its parts are many, they form one body. So it is with Christ. . . .

Now the body is not made up of one part but of many. If the foot should say, "Because I am not a hand, I do not belong to the body," it would not for that reason cease to be part of the body. And if the ear should say, "Because I am an eye, I do not belong to the body," it would not for that reason cease to be a part of the body. If the whole body were an eye, where would the sense of hearing be? If the whole body were an ear, where would the sense of smell be? (1 Corinthians 12:14–17)

Paul says that we, as Christians, are all one "unit," even though we're made up of many "parts." None of us—students included—can say, "Well, I don't really want to be accountable to those people, so I just won't be a part of that unit." When we become believers, we become a part of the body of Christ. End of story. And that throws our lot in with other Christians forever. Which is a good thing. We need the other parts of the body in order to function and grow. If I am an eye without an ear, how can I hear? If I am an ear without a nose, how can I smell?

We ask our students, "What would happen to your hand if it decided it did not need any input or help from the rest of the body?" Without the arm, the hand can't function. Without the brain, the hand can't function. Without the heart, the hand can't function. The implication is clear: Without the rest of the body, that hand, at the very least, would never fulfill its purpose; at worst, it would be rendered useless. The same applies to each of our students. They need the rest of the body of Christ in order to find and fulfill their God-given purpose.

This is a critical point for teenagers who want to become students of influence. They need one another. We illustrate this point by asking, "What happens when you stub your big toe on the bedpost in the middle of the night?" Probably something like this: Nerves in the big toe send a signal to the brain, reporting pain in the South Pole region. The brain immediately sends out an all-points bulletin. The eyes respond by tearing up. The mouth and vocal chords respond by screaming (we won't try to guess *what*). The hand responds by grabbing the toe. The good leg responds by jumping up and down. And all these things happen in a matter of split seconds! All the parts of the body respond to the need of the one part.

Students who refuse to establish strong accountability relationships are like a big toe that has no one to care for it when it is injured. They are like a hand that decides it does not need input or help from the rest of the body. They risk a life of loneliness, pain, spiritual impotence, and zero influence with their peers.

Common sense argues for accountability.

It is a fact of life that we all do better when someone is checking up on us. In almost every facet of life, what is *expected* is connected to what is *inspected*.

Several soccer seasons ago, Stuart saw this truth develop in an unforgettable way:

My son Grant was playing his first season of soccer, and I was no help to him at all. Soccer was a sissy sport when I was growing up. I knew nothing about the game. But Grant seemed to be having an OK time anyway. Not really great, but not really bad either.

One weekend a good friend of ours who plays professional baseball came to town for a three-game series against the Braves. Grant had a soccer game that Saturday morning, and when our friend heard about it, he called and asked for directions to the soccer field so he could watch Grant play.

Now understand: Grant thinks this guy hung the moon. Grant's room is full of autographed baseballs and baseball cards from him.

I didn't tell Grant about the call. I decided to surprise him.

Grant played the first half of the game in his usual hesitant way—not very confident or aggressive. But just as the second half started, our friend arrived. Grant saw him as he walked around the field, and a miraculous transformation occurred: Grant became Pele! He played the game of his life—aggressive, great defense, even headed the ball a few times. I watched with my mouth open. And then I picked up on something: Grant kept looking over at our friend on the sidelines to make sure he was watching. His performance was at its peak because someone he cared about was checking up on him.

Think about it this way: Would students study hard if there were no tests? (Maybe that's not a good illustration.) Would athletes practice as hard if the coach just handed them the balls and sent them out to practice without him? We all know the answer to that; just watch any PE class in middle school.

We definitely do better when we know someone is checking up on us.

Chinks in the Armor

Common sense argues for accountability for another reason: We all have weaknesses—"chinks in our armor," so to speak. And those weaknesses *will* be made known in one of two ways: Either someone who cares about us will point out our shortcomings to us, or our shortcomings will wind up being exposed in public. Every weakness will manifest itself eventually. The question for our students is, how do they want a particular weakness to be exposed?

If our students are going to be influential, they must have strong accountability relationships with friends who care enough about them to speak up about their weaknesses before someone else does. Hearing something negative from a friend is tough, but the alternative—hearing it from someone else, perhaps in an embarrassing public moment—is a whole lot more painful. Teenagers like to tell one another, "I've got your back." Our students need friends who will do exactly that.

We like to remind students of Paul's challenge to Christians to put on the full armor of God. In Ephesians 6:13–17, Paul tells us to put on the belt of truth, the breastplate of righteousness, the shield of faith, and the helmet of salvation; to fit our feet with readiness; and to pick up the sword of the Spirit. (To illustrate this concept, we have gone so far as to dress up a student in a weight belt, a catcher's chest protector, a garbage can lid, a football helmet, combat boots, and a toy sword.) In practical terms, these pieces of armor defend the midsection, torso, feet, and head—basically the entire front portion of the body. But that leaves one critical area exposed: the back. And that's where most of the enemy's attacks will come from: the back, where we're not looking.

Therein lies the beauty of God's design for accountability: When our students enter into accountability relationships with other Christians, they stand back to back with one another. No area is exposed to the enemy. They can see the attacks coming at each other's backs and head them off. They can cover the chinks in one another's armor.

It's All about the Experience

Another reason why accountability makes sense is that it allows us to learn from the experiences of others. Our students need to be in relationship with people who are winning the war and not getting hammered. They need to surround themselves with friends who've had battle experience and have learned from their mistakes—friends who have developed spiritual maturity in an area or areas where our students are weak. Such friends will be more apt to be sensitive in confrontation. They are likely to be less cocky or conceited and more sensitive to their own weaknesses. Paul alluded to this type of person when he wrote to the Galatian church: "Brothers, if someone is caught in a sin, you who are spiritual should restore him gently. But watch yourself, or you also may be tempted. Carry each other's burdens, and in this way you will fulfill the law of Christ" (Galatians 6:1–2).

The ability to restore someone gently is a byproduct of spiritual maturity. That means that, in order for our students to experience gentle restoration in areas where they fail, they must seek out experienced, spiritually mature accountability partners. This may mean choosing partners who are older than they are—possibly adults. It may also mean that they choose to be accountable to different people on different issues. For example, one person may hold them accountable for their quiet times, another for their entertainment choices, another for their relationships with unbelieving friends, and so on.

Accountability and Max Q

Nowhere is accountability more important than in that last area: relationships with unbelieving friends. That is the context in which Max Q is the strongest. And just as the space shuttle must have astronauts and a control center constantly evaluating and double checking each other as they monitor all the gauges, systems, and inner workings of the spacecraft, so must our students have someone—or several someones—constantly monitoring and evaluating their friendships with unbelievers.

Why is this important? Investing in someone who needs Christ can be a consuming task for our students. Depending on the intellectual, emotional, and spiritual distance an unbelieving friend has to come in order to trust in Christ, such a relationship can be spiritually, emotionally, and even physically draining. Our students need someone to warn them when the relationship begins to take a negative and dangerous toll. They need an accountability partner in place whose mission it is to constantly examine their minds, hearts, and motivation.

The truth is, without accountability our students don't have much chance of making it through spiritual Max Q. Their convictions will begin to break apart. Their priorities gauge will malfunction, and there will be no one to notice the change. Eventually they will succumb to the influence of their unbelieving friend—a tragedy that could have been avoided if strong accountability had been established and maintained.

What would happen if we had more accountability in the body of Christ? Fewer dads would hit the road for good if they would seek out other men with whom they could talk openly about their frustrations in marriage and temptations at the office. Fewer moms would have affairs if they would develop relationships with other women who would ask them hard questions about their security, self-esteem, and pent-up anger. And fewer students, after starting a relationship with a lost peer with the greatest of intentions, would drift into a lifestyle contrary to the heart of God if they would only give someone permission to question them about that friendship.

Clearly, accountability is in our students' best interest. So why, with all the positive ramifications of accountability, do they still resist it? In a word: confrontation. Students resist accountability because they hate confrontation.

Acceptance at All Costs

This is really a problem for all of us. We don't like to confront someone because we are more concerned about what that person thinks about us than we are about his or her spiritual life. We don't develop a true accountability relationship because we want to maintain our friendship at all costs. We don't want to build up and strengthen our friend at the risk of having that person be unhappy with us.

Coach Mike Krzyzewski relates a story that illustrates this principle beautifully. Two of his freshman players, Johnny Dawkins and Mark Alerie, were late for a team bus. Coach K remembers: "We didn't know where they were, they had not called, and every other member of the team was on time. So we left them behind. Eventually the two caught up with us, and I remember being ready to hammer them. But after hearing that they had overslept, I began to wonder why other members of our team had not checked up on them."[2] I can tell you why the other teammates didn't check on them: They didn't want to make those guys (Dawkins and Alerie) mad at them for waking them up! They were more concerned about the friendship than they were the friend.

We talk about this principle in great detail in *The Seven Checkpoints*, but it is worth repeating here: A true friend is one who will *love* you, not just *accept* you. You can accept someone without truly loving that person. In a friendship where acceptance is the priority, confrontation rarely happens. Neither friend is willing to take the risk of saying the things that need to be said.

Students need to recognize that a true friend is someone who accepts them just as they are, but who loves them too much to leave them that way. Think of the tragic deaths of comedians John Candy, Chris Farley, and John Belushi. How many times did we hear people on TV claim, "Oh, he was one of my best friends"? Yet they never confronted their "best friend" on his alcohol, food, or drug abuse. They chose to ignore these obvious danger signals for the sake of being accepted by their famous buddy. Apparently they were more committed to the friendship than the friend.

Direction, Not Perfection

Another reason students don't confront is because, in their minds, their own spiritual lives disqualify them. Teenagers often have a more truthful perspective on themselves than anyone else does. They are keenly aware of their shortcomings and feel disqualified to confront others based on a perceived lack of leverage to do so.

Our students need to understand that accountability does not demand perfection. It is not at all about living a life void of mistakes. If that were the case, why would any of us need to be accountable to anyone? I once heard NFL great and future Hall of Fame wide receiver Jerry Rice say that the reason he has continued to play, despite reaching an age at which most football players retire, is that he is still in pursuit of the perfect game. Well, Jerry will never be able to retire, because the perfect game will never happen! And if students wait to be perfect before they enter into an accountability relationship, *that* will never happen either.

The Christian life is a lifelong journey of walking in a certain direction, falling down, getting up, dusting ourselves off, and walking on, mile after mile after mile. It is a life of direction aimed at perfection—not the converse. The major factor in accountability is not that any of us is perfect; it's that the course of our lives is set in the right direction.

The Root of Pride

Still another reason students resist confrontation is, quite simply, pride. As we are all very aware, pride is powerful—and lethal. Pride can propel a teenager to great heights and accomplishments when properly appropriated. It can also drive a student to his or her own destruction when mishandled. Pride looms large in our students' resistance to accountability. Yet it is pride's destructive power that is the very reason accountability is so important in their lives.

Relative Truth

Finally, students often refuse to confront because they don't want to be accused of being judgmental. Relative thought has so infiltrated modern youth culture that students today equate confronting with judging. They reason, "Since faith is an individual journey, how can I confront you about what you believe to be true? If it is true for you, then I have to accept that. Who am I to judge?"

Here is a piece of liberating, yet responsible, news for you to share with your students: There is a standard of absolute truth—God and his Word—and that Word commands Christians to judge one another. Judging nonbelievers is off-limits, but we have a responsibility to each other. This is not a man-made idea for exerting moral control; it is God's design for his body. Postmodern thinkers can protest all they want, but the fact remains that God intends for Christians to be accountable to one another. The survival of our core students in the midst of Max Q depends upon it.

Making Accountability a Reality

So now we get to where the rubber meets the road: How do we as youth ministers help our students develop accountability relationships?

Find the Right Person

We ask students to begin this process by praying that God will lead them to the right person or persons. Then we tell them to consider these factors:

Choose someone you can meet with on a consistent basis.

Consistent, face-to-face interaction is crucial for effective accountability. Because my accountability partner and I both have very busy schedules, it would be so easy to let other important things crowd out our time together. But our accountability relationship is a priority for both of us. I suppose we could try to hold one another accountable through occasional phone calls or e-mail, but those methods are not nearly as effective as face-to-face contact. We figure that not meeting together on a consistent basis is like a team that goes out to play its games without ever getting together to practice first. That's no way to win!

The lives of today's teenagers are as hectic (if not more so) than ours. For our students, finding the time to meet with an accountability partner can be as difficult as finding a sumo wrestler's belly button. We need to convince them that it's worth the effort. We encourage our students to choose a weekly time and place to meet—and to keep the date. Accountability must become such a priority in their lives that they will allow nothing to jeopardize meeting together on a consistent basis.

Choose someone you can trust completely.

I heard Oprah Winfrey say recently, "When someone shows you who they really are—believe them." She's actually on to something that is critical to the process of accountability: trust. Students need to be able to trust that their accountability partner will believe them when they open up and reveal who they really are. If a person cannot be trusted, however, then he or she is disqualified from being in that kind of relationship. This is not to say that trust can't be developed, but it does imply that a high level of trust must pre-exist before an effective accountability relationship can be entered into.

After all, trust is the currency of relationship; it's what allows authenticity and vulnerability to emerge. Without trust, these characteristics will struggle to appear. And if they don't become a part of the fabric of an accountability relationship, then the accountability of that relationship will be ineffective at best.

Choose someone to hold you accountable—not someone for you to hold accountable.

The primary question for our students is not "Who can I hold accountable?" It's "Who can hold *me* accountable?" Pursuing accountability on the basis of the first question leads students down a one-way street that is intended to be two-way. Effective accountability is a partnership of trust, not a dictatorship. Asking the correct question will cause students to gravitate toward an accountability partner who upholds the standards they desire to maintain in their own lives—someone who desires the same depth of relationship with Christ and the same level of influence with unbelieving peers.

Deferring to a weaker believer in accountability is the equivalent of a great football team playing down to the level of its competition. Sometimes it can even be dangerous. As we said earlier, developing an accountability relationship is the equivalent of going to war with someone and fighting back to back with that person. You want to know that he or she is well trained, battle ready, and as anxious to stay alive as you are. To be matched with anyone else could be fatal! The same holds true for our students: Having the wrong person holding them accountable—someone who is not vigilant, or not battle tested, or not willing to choose the friend over the friendship— could be hazardous to their spiritual health.

Choose someone of the same gender.

It constantly amazes us that so many small groups in youth ministries across America are coed. There is nothing more dangerous or inherently ineffective than accountability between students of the opposite sex. For one thing, authenticity is hard to develop, because hormones and attraction disguise themselves as trust. And the fact is, the desire for acceptance is at its peak in guy-girl relationships. Trust can't be built if students are simply "performing" to gain acceptance.

For another thing, guys and girls generally struggle with different issues. We guarantee the guys in a coed group will get frustrated quickly listening to a young lady talk about her constant struggle with self-esteem. Seemingly never-ending conversations about waistlines and pimples will get old more than fast! Conversely, the girls in a coed group will never want to date boys again when they hear how often their brothers in Christ struggle with their thoughts.

The bottom line is that effective accountability is intended to be a deeply meaningful, spiritual experience. Too many times we have seen a guy and girl turn accountability into romance, simply because they entered into deep, meaningful conversation on the pretext of accountability. Holding hands to pray quickly became holding hands to play.

Choose someone who is spiritually stronger than you are.

When it comes to finding an accountability partner, we challenge our students to seek out someone who is spiritually stronger than they are. Todd and Lee, for example, are two guys who've been meeting for several years with Roger, a man ten-plus years their senior. Two female students, Chandler and Mary, meet consistently with Stuart's wife, Kellee. Why? Because learning from the life experiences of Roger and Kellee plays to their advantage. These students have set a high bar for themselves, and they understand that they will rise to the level of expectation in their lives. The accountability they receive from these "older" friends helps them accomplish their purpose.

Determine the Area of Accountability

In addition to finding the right person to hold them accountable, our students need to pinpoint the area or areas in which they desire accountability. This decision can actually help them choose the right partner, since they can make the choice based on their particular needs. A friend will probably not be much help in an area if he or she has the same struggle.

Once the area of accountability has been identified, our students need to explain their situations in detail to their partner, particularly as they relate to the friends they are trying to influence for Christ. By sharing their weaknesses or temptations in an area, along with who they are trying to reach, how they intend to reach them, and what dangerous environments they're likely to encounter in the process, students create a playing field and a strategy for accountability. They also give their partner the information necessary to pray effectively.

Our students must not be so arrogant as to think they can reach their unbelieving peers on their own. They absolutely need a partner or partners who will monitor their lives while they reach out to their lost friends. Remember, marines go in as teams, never solo. Jesus sent the disciples out in pairs. Likewise, our students need someone to hold on to their ankles and strap them down while they reach over the fence into a lost world.

A Signature under the Surface

In Japan a crafter of archery bows will always sign and date each bow inside the top layer of lamination. The crafter's name isn't visible, since that would be considered immodest in Japanese culture. You can only find out who made a particular bow if it breaks. Then you can peel back the laminate layer and see the name. If the bow failed due to poor craftsmanship, the crafter is held responsible.

Accountability is critical to our students becoming influential, and it must be taken seriously. The accountability relationships our students establish become signatures under the surface of their lives. If our students break under the pressure, who's name will be visible? Yours?

The potential to break will always be there. But by having the names of experienced, spiritually mature craftsmen and craftswomen written under the surface, our students will have the best chance of coming out intact, even under the pressure of Max Q.

Pressure Points

1. Read Luke 17:3–5. Is your response to accountability the same as the disciples' response? Why or why not?

2. Read 1 Corinthians 12:12–20. Can you think of an instance in your life when you would have been saved a world of pain if you had allowed the body of Christ to be the body of Christ (that is, if you had allowed other Christians to care for you and hold you accountable)? Explain.

3. Discuss this statement with your leadership team: "Your relationship with God is personal—but not private."

4. Do you have anyone at this point in your life who is holding you accountable? If so, in what areas?

5. Would you say that your youth ministry has developed a culture of accountability? Why or why not?

There is the great lesson of
"Beauty and the Beast";
that a thing must be loved
before it is loveable.

G. K. Chesterton

The Unconditional-Acceptance Principle

Out-Loving the World

Teenagers don't really choose their friends. They simply gravitate toward those peers who accept them. It's as if they have a built-in acceptance radar: They are drawn toward people and environments of acceptance.

Because this principle is true, we probably need to edit the parental jargon that advises "Choose your friends wisely" or "Be careful who you hang out with." Students don't really choose their friends. Their friends choose them.

Think about it. Teenagers don't set up a table in the high-school foyer on the first day of their freshman year with a big sign that reads Accepting Applications for Friends Here! Students don't "try out" friends the way athletes try out for

171

the football or volleyball team. Those whom students build relationships with has more to do with who is willing to accept them than who matches up to a predetermined checklist of desirable characteristics.

Acceptance is an incredibly powerful desire in all human beings. It causes men and women alike to abandon their integrity and convictions. For teenagers this desire is magnified tenfold. Acceptance is so powerful in the lives of students that it transcends and overrides any person or group of people. It trumps integrity, convictions, and the welfare of the very people from whom acceptance is sought. For teens acceptance by a friend is more important than the friend. When students think acceptance is at stake, there is almost nothing they won't do.

The Critical Link

Acceptance and influence are inexorably linked. Within a relationship, you can't have sustained influence apart from acceptance. Students resist the influence of those adults and peers they perceive do not accept them. When they feel accepted, however, they drop their guard.

Every student pastor, youth worker, and parent—along with every developing student of influence—must keep this principle at the epicenter of everything they do. As Christians we must become the most accepting people and provide the most accepting environments a lost student can possibly experience. To be influential we must out-accept the competition. Many teenagers with less-than-desirable lifestyles and belief systems are out there right now, accepting lost teenagers. Our students cannot allow unbelieving teens to out-love and out-accept them.

Failing When It Counts

The fact is, lost teenagers won't embrace our message until they feel assured of our love and acceptance. We are failing in this regard in the church. Too often we are more committed to being right than to developing relationships with people who need the hope we have in Jesus Christ. We want our position recognized more than we want to build a relational bridge. And because we're afraid that showing unconditional love equals agreement with sin, we are conditioning our students to be like us: judgmental rather than accepting. The result is the exact opposite of what we want if our goal is to develop students and ministries of influence.

Students not only gravitate toward acceptance; they flee people and environments of rejection. Nothing hurts like rejection. Teenagers will go to extreme measures to avoid it. We know of a church that used to measure the length of the shorts of every girl who attempted to enter the youth room. If the shorts were too short, the girl didn't get in. Students avoided this church like the plague.

Could it be that the reason lost teenagers resist the evangelistic efforts of the church is that they sense rejection from us? Imagine, the very entity and environment that should be the most loving and accepting is viewed by the modern student culture as the most unloving and rejecting! Often those students who decide to give church a try act up—either consciously or subconsciously—simply to gauge how much we care. And if we fail the test, they flee. They're gone and so is our opportunity to influence them for Christ.

Becoming a Gravitational Force

The importance of acceptance to influence is glaringly obvious:

- If friends determine the direction and quality of a teenager's life and . . .

- If teenagers develop friendships based on who makes them feel accepted, then . . .

- The people who make them feel accepted will eventually become their friends and will impact the direction and quality of their lives.

That means that our students must become the gravitational force in their lost friends' lives. Their acceptance must be stronger than anyone else's. Their friendship must matter more than anyone else's. Almost all the teenagers we know who have placed their faith in Christ and have begun to walk with him consistently have had a Christian friend walking beside them, encouraging them every step of the way. That's disciplism, and it's impossible to accomplish without acceptance.

For teenagers, the arena of acceptance is a place of maximum dynamic pressure. It's a battleground—one on which students and ministries of influence must win.

The Big Easy

Clay and Mary, two Christian college students from our church, were on a trip to New Orleans with Clay's fraternity when their moment of truth came knocking. Or should we say screaming. As they were walking through the French Quarter, they came upon a "street preacher." He was standing next to a large wooden cross and shouting a message of repentance and judgment at the top of his lungs. Clay and Mary listened intently for a few moments. They noticed that while the man's words were true, his presentation seemed to lack relevance. It offended more people than it compelled. Many bystanders laughed at his antics. Some stopped to listen out of curiosity. Most simply ignored him and walked on.

As Clay and Mary walked away, they began to converse about the effectiveness of this preacher's method for reaching others with the Good News. Neither questioned his heart. Neither questioned his passion. And neither questioned his message. What bothered them was his approach. It was his means to the end that seemed to sit in their souls like an early morning meal of Mexican food.

Perhaps what made it such a heavy lump was their own reason for being there. They were both strong believers and leaders in our church. They were both committed to making God's name and fame great on their campus at Georgia Tech. They were both members of the Greek system, and they were both personally, intentionally connected with students of questionable lifestyles and habits for the purpose of influencing them for Christ. They were in New Orleans and the French Quarter (not exactly the holiest of places) for the express purpose of continuing to build relationships with their lost friends.

Can you imagine the spiritual frustration involved in investing in college students who are hellbent on having the time of their lives while in school? The maximum dynamic pressure of such a mission is incalculable. Clay and Mary understand Max Q all too well! They came home from their experience in New Orleans wondering internally and aloud: Is there a "best way" to influence others for Christ?

The Most Excellent Way

According to Scripture, the answer is yes. There *is* a best way to live a life of standards, priorities, and accountability—and a life that will have a positive, powerful influence on others. Paul calls it the "most excellent way" in his letter to the Corinthian church: "And now I will show you the most excellent way" (1 Corinthians 12:31).

This sentence, interestingly enough, follows a discussion on spiritual gifts and the different parts of the body of Christ. You get the sense that the Corinthian Christians were struggling with the idea that everyone has different gifts and brings different strengths (and weaknesses) to the church. Apparently many people were competing to be considered the more "important" parts.

When Paul mentions "the most excellent way" (sounds like Wayne and Garth from *Wayne's World*), he is referring to the right way for believers to exercise spiritual gifts. He does not identify love as a gift. Rather, love is a fruit of the Spirit— and it supercedes the gifts of the Spirit. The implication here is huge: A believer can't use the gift of prophecy as an excuse to speak and act condescendingly and harshly toward others. The spiritual gift of evangelism does not free its recipient from showing unconditional love.

Our students need to understand that love always trumps any giftings they may have. It overrides any mission that they (or we as their youth ministers) seek to accomplish. Zeal to see lost teenagers come to faith in Christ must never take precedence over the love we are to display in the process. We have made this mistake for far too long in youth ministry. We have conditioned our students to take pride in words spoken in scrutiny and judgment—words that should have been spoken in love and acceptance. No wonder lost teenagers run.

Word Power

For students to become influential with their peers, they must learn to leverage their words. Paul speaks to this when he says, "Do not let any unwholesome talk come out of your mouths, but only what is helpful for building others up according to their needs, that it may benefit those who listen" (Ephesians 4:29).

The picture here is of a screen over our mouths—a restraining leash on our tongues. Our students must restrain themselves from speaking words that are "unwholesome"— literally, words that are "rotten, unfit for use, potentially damaging." Just as a pit bull will attack if his leash is removed, so our students' tongues—because they are a "restless evil" (James 3:8)—will do damage if they're allowed to.

By starting with restraint, however, our students can leverage their words for good in the lives of their friends. The question they must ask themselves is, "Will the words I'm about to speak build this person up or tear this person down?" The issue is motivation. Unconditional acceptance calls for our students to speak from hearts that are more interested in helping than hurting, more interested in loving than judging.

The Truth-Love Connection

In fact, Paul tells us in Ephesians 4:15 to speak "the truth in love." The implication is that truth can be told in a way that will either help or hurt others. There are no neutral words. Listeners deposit every word spoken to them in one of two banks: hurtful or helpful. By speaking the truth in love—by only speaking words that build up rather than tear down—our students can accumulate spiritual collateral in their lost friends' lives. Eventually they will be able to draw upon this collateral as leverage for influence.

It is this idea that motivates Paul to write these words:

If I speak with human eloquence and angelic ecstasy but don't love, I'm nothing but the creaking of a rusty gate. If I speak God's Word with power, revealing all his mysteries and making everything as plain as day, and if I have faith that says to a mountain, "Jump," and it jumps, but I don't love, I'm nothing. If I give everything I own to the poor and even go the stake to be burned as a martyr, but I don't love, I've gotten nowhere. So no matter what I say, what I believe, and what I do, I'm bankrupt without love. (1 Corinthians 13:1–3 *The Message Remix*)

Without love, every word that our students speak to their friends is irrelevant. There is an old adage that says, "People don't care what you know until they know that you care." Our students discount and discredit all that they know about God and his love when they don't exemplify that love in their lives. When students proclaim that they love God but refuse to unconditionally accept those he has made in his image, it causes a disconnect of monumental proportions. It unplugs their influence.

The Choice

Many students argue that they just can't do it: They can't love unconditionally. It's unnatural to them. It's a struggle. They don't feel like accepting their lost peers. But there is a major flaw in their line of thinking.

Stuart's dad had a massive heart attack several years ago. He survived, but since then he has faced the toughest task of his life: coping mentally with his mortality after his near-brush with death. Doctors have said that the best thing he can do for his heart is to exercise. But if you're a victim of a heart attack, that recommendation seems counterintuitive. You live with the ever-constant realization that your heart is weak. And you have the ever-constant fear that physical exertion will bring on another attack. That's why many heart patients don't follow their doctor's orders to get the exercise they need.

You don't exercise your heart because *it is* in shape; you exercise your heart *to get it* in shape. What do you say to a man who doesn't like to exercise because he has a weak heart and no energy? "When your heart is strong, exercise"? No, you say, "Exercise, and your heart will become strong."

Like physical exercise, spiritual exercise is an act of the

will—a feeling-defying act of the will. You force yourself to exercise. You force yourself to love. It's a choice.

Students may object, "Well, I'm just not a very accepting person." But that's no excuse to reject the unlovable.

They may say, "I just don't love easily." But that's no excuse to be judgmental and harsh.

They may say, "I have a hard time giving." But that's no excuse to be selfish with their time, energy, and heart.

The assumption behind such statements is this: "If my heart ever changes, then I will start unconditionally loving and accepting my lost friend." That's like saying, "Well, if I ever wake up with the energy to exercise, I'll start exercising. If I wake up with a smaller appetite, I'll eat less. If I wake up and find I've lost my taste for ice cream, I'll cut back on Dairy Queen."

Students may say, "I don't feel like loving." Well, no one ever feels like exercising in the beginning, but eventually they do. The key is making the decision and getting started.

Or they say, "I tried. It didn't do any good. My lost friend is still lost." That reminds me of my habit of doing five hundred crunches every once in a while and then running to the mirror to see if I have six-pack abs. Getting in shape takes place with consistency and persistence over time. So does loving.

Unconditional acceptance doesn't come naturally to our selfish hearts. We just have to do it. And over time our hearts heal and become strong. The longer our students have been judging and criticizing their lost peers, the harder they will have to work to begin exercising unconditional acceptance. The longer a heart has been neglected, the harder it is to get it in shape.

The key is to make the choice. Contrary to everything you might hear on *As the World Turns,* we don't *fall* in love; we *choose* to love, and then we do what it takes to start loving. Jesus didn't fall to earth, say "uh-oh," and decide that he would die on the cross for humanity. Jesus didn't fall in love with humanity. From the beginning of time, he *chose* to love mankind and to die for our sins and for his Father's glory. His love was a choice. Love is a choice for our students too.

Love Is . . .

Paul spends time in his letter to the church in Corinth helping them understand what love is and what it is not:

> Love never gives up. Love cares more for others than for self. Love doesn't want what it doesn't have. Love doesn't strut, doesn't have a swelled head, doesn't force itself on others, isn't always "me first," doesn't fly off the handle, doesn't keep score of the sins of others, doesn't revel when others grovel, takes pleasure in the flowering of truth, puts up with anything, trusts God always, always looks for the best, never looks back, but keeps going to the end. Love never dies. (1 Corinthians 13:4–8 *The Message Remix*)

Love serves. Love endures. Love is sacrificial. Love shares. Obviously, choosing this kind of love is not easy. To love people who don't live by our standards and belief system is a difficult decision to make—and an even harder one to carry out. But there is a major principle here that our students must understand:

You can't express or experience unconditional love unless you are with people and in environments that are inconsistent and different from you.

This principle is at the root of our salvation. When we were inconsistent with God, he did not deny us, change his expectation of us, or modify his evaluation of us. No, God through Jesus Christ chose to love us despite our inconsistencies and differences with himself.

What's the Difference?

A student's lost friends *will* be different. Their lives *will* be inconsistent with Christian values and beliefs. That's what makes the choice to love and accept them unconditionally so difficult—and so necessary.

Unfortunately, in relationships with peers who don't know Christ, students often fail to make that choice. They have a tendency to be "an eye for an eye, a tooth for a tooth" kind of people:

- If you reject me, then I'll reject you.

- If you don't come to my church, then I'm not going to come to your deal.

- If you don't return my calls, I'm going to stop trying to reach you.

- If you don't express interest in my stuff, then I won't express interest in your stuff.

How easy it is for our students to devolve into this kind of thinking! The problem is, if they go with their natural tendencies, they will end up treating their lost friends the way those friends treat them—or worse.

When Jesus came into the world, the "eye for an eye" kind of thinking was the normal way for people to respond in relationships. It was even taught by many of the teachers of that day: If someone mistreats you, you mistreat that person back. If someone is good to you, you be good to that person in return. You may forgive someone three times, but no one can expect you to forgive four, five, or six times. Love the people that love you and hate the people you consider your enemies.

That was the relational standard of the culture until Jesus showed up and changed everything:

> You have heard that it was said, "Love your neighbor and hate your enemy." But I tell you: Love your enemies and pray for those who persecute you, that you may be sons of your Father in heaven. He causes his sun to rise on the evil and the good, and sends rain on the righteous and the unrighteous. If you love those who love you, what reward will you get? Are not even the tax collectors doing that? And if you greet only your brothers, what are you doing more than others? Do not even pagans do that? Be perfect, therefore, as your heavenly Father is perfect. (Matthew 5:43–48)

Jesus points out that we are not as different from unbelievers as we think we are. The sun rises on the lost and the found. Rain falls on the Christian student and the unbelieving student. We all have been created in the image of God.

He also implies that showing unconditional acceptance only to those people whose lives are consistent with our own is no credit to us. Even tax collectors (who were the worst of the worst in Jesus' day) love those who love them, he notes. And if the only people we accept are our brothers and sisters, then we are not really very accepting, are we? Even pagans do that much.

In other words, Jesus confirms the principle we stated earlier: We can't express or experience unconditional love unless we are with people and in environments that are inconsistent or different from us. He connects perfection with our ability to overlook inconsistencies, overcome personal differences, and unconditionally love all the people in our lives.

Truth be told, most of our students are more concerned with living comfortably than loving and accepting their friends unconditionally. In order to be students of influence, however, they will have to answer this question in the affirmative: "Are you willing to express unconditional love to those people within your sphere of influence who are different from you and whose lives are inconsistent with yours?"

The Ministry of Reconciliation

Our students need to answer yes, because they have been given the same ministry that Christ had while he was on earth. Paul writes:

All this is from God, who reconciled us to himself through Christ and gave us the ministry of reconciliation: that God was reconciling the world to himself in

Christ, not counting men's sins against them. And he has committed to us the message of reconciliation. We are therefore Christ's ambassadors, as though God were making his appeal through us. We implore you on Christ's behalf: Be reconciled to God. God made him who had no sin to be sin for us, so that in him we might become the righteousness of God. (2 Corinthians 5:18–21)

Reconciliation means "making two conflicting things compatible." And that's our students' job: to make their lost friends, who are in conflict with God because of their sin, compatible with God. Our students' unconditional acceptance of their friends is the relational bridge that connects one side to the other and allows reconciliation to occur.

Our students need to remember that when they became Christians, God did something incredible. They didn't do anything; God did. He single-handedly cleared away everything that blocked the way for them to be in relationship with him. He didn't wait for them to deal with their sin on their own. (If he had, he would still be waiting.) No, God did it all. He changed our students to make them compatible to himself.

Why then do students think they have to wait for their peers to change before they offer their friendship? They do the opposite of what the ministry of reconciliation calls them to do. Their message to their friends goes like this: "I've got great news! You can be reconciled to God. You just can't be reconciled to me. God has forgiven you of all your sins, and he wants a relationship with you. But I haven't forgiven you for your differences and your inconsistencies, and you can't have a relationship with me. You see, I have a higher standard than God."

When students take this approach, they are refusing to do for their friends what God in Christ has done for them. And they reveal to the world that they really don't understand and appreciate their own salvation.

Clarifying the Goal

For our students the goal of reconciliation is to develop a relationship built upon acceptance—despite a friend's past. Despite a friend's lifestyle. Despite a friend's flawed ideas about or disagreements with God. Reconciliation is about compatibility, not conformity. Making two conflicting things compatible does not require making them conform first. To think otherwise is like thinking you have to get in the shower and clean up before you can get in the shower and clean up.

We teach our students this simple formula:

Reconciliation + Relationship = Influence

Our students' willingness to love and accept their friends unconditionally is the one thing that paves the way to reconciliation, relationship, and ultimately influence for the sake of Christ. Yes, reconciliation can be messy. Reconciliation takes time. It can be all-consuming. But it—not judgment—must be the goal. Our students have been given a ministry as Christ's ambassadors. God is making his appeal through them. And that means, as our friend David Crowder says, his love needs to be "big and loud" in their lives.

Creating Safe Environments

Put down this book right now and hightail it to your nearest pet store. Purchase a turtle and bring it home. Now hand the turtle over to a few children and watch to see if the turtle will stick its head out. My kids thought they had gotten a defective turtle when they found one in the woods behind our home. Why? The turtle would never stick its head out of its shell. But who could blame the turtle? It was being poked at with sticks, pencils, and whatever else the kids could find in an attempt to make it reveal its face. Who wouldn't hide?

As youth leaders we can learn a lesson from turtles. When a turtle doesn't feel safe, it retreats to the comfort and protection of its shell. The only time it will stick its head out is when it perceives that the environment is safe enough to do so. A wise turtle-owner will get a box, fill it with grass, add a small bowl of water, and wait. Over time the turtle will learn to trust the safety of the environment, and it will reveal its head.

Poking and prodding a teenager, just like poking and prodding a turtle, is counterproductive. The more we press lost teenagers about faith issues, the deeper those teens will retreat.

Lanny Donoho, director of BigStuf Camps in Alpharetta, Georgia, is a master at creating the kind of environments in which lost students slowly but surely come to the understanding that they're safe, that it's OK to be vulnerable. Lanny's programming is strategic for this purpose. By the middle of a typical week at camp, students who arrived with a chip on their shoulder feel the freedom to let their guard down, "come out of their shells," and get real with the deep issues of their lives. From the outset, Lanny doesn't poke and prod. He simply presents an environment of acceptance and love.

Our students must do the same thing. They must make their relationships safe havens for their lost friends. Only in an environment of acceptance will their friends be willing to open up about their lives and seriously consider the message of reconciliation.

Carrying the Load

As we said, reconciliation can be messy. Acceptance means dirt and all. It's very possible that our students will have to shoulder the weight of consequences and complications that result from their lost friend's sin. They may have to clean up some messes. They will certainly have to deal with the ramifications of their friend's irresponsibility and inconsistency. Add to these things the fact that other Christians will probably make fun of them for being in relationship with someone who screws up. And then consider that their friend may never acknowledge their deep sacrifice and unconditional love.

Reconciliation is definitely a straight shot to Max Q.

Yet in the process, our students will be paving the way to influence. And they will be following the example of Jesus. Paul puts it this way: "God made him who had no sin to be sin for us, so that in him we might become the righteousness of God" (2 Corinthians 5:21). Jesus became sin for us. He took the burden of our sin and the consequences of our sin and shouldered the weight so that you and I can have a relationship with God.

Acceptance and love are the way of Christ. They are also the way of students and ministries of influence.

Checking the Love Quotient

Do your students unconditionally accept their lost peers? How can you evaluate how well your students and your ministry are doing in this area?

What makes these questions so hard to answer is the fact that our mission as youth ministers is not really tangible. In fact, we would go so far as to say this: If you can apply a tangible standard of measurement to your mission, you are probably veering away from disciplism. A disciplism standard is always going to be a little fuzzy, because relationships—not numbers—are the factors in play.

Let's face it. Our tendency is to count stuff—money, fannies in the pews, baptisms, membership, attendance. You name it, we count it. And if the numbers are going up, then we consider that we are accomplishing our mission.

But this evaluation tool (counting) has a major flaw. When you are dealing with a living organism like the church, and you are talking about relationships driven by unconditional acceptance and love, then counting is not the best way to get a true indication of what is going on. Think about it: My family is a living organism. If you were to ask me how my family is doing, I would not look at you and say, "Great! There are five of us!" The number of people in my family tells you nothing about the health of my family.

This is an important point, because ministries that evaluate success by the numbers usually don't recognize when they have veered off course. Your ministry could operate under a facade of success for years. All the parents are happy. Your pastor loves you. Your students are good kids. The numbers are up. But if you haven't developed students of influence who can withstand the pressure of Max Q, you are nowhere near reaching your goal.

What we establish as our evaluation tool determines what we focus on as a target. If we want to have ministries of influence, we need to make sure we don't set up an evaluation tool that pulls us away from the target of developing students who unconditionally accept their peers.

Ten Questions for Evaluating Acceptance

We have come up with ten questions that serve as a grid for evaluating how well our students and ministries are doing in the area of unconditional acceptance. These are questions that must be asked often. They must be answered with all honesty and candor. Failure to consistently face the truth about the love quotient in our students and ministries will absolutely paralyze our influence.

1. Are we being true to God's Word?

This may not seem like a relationship question, but it's really the only logical place to start. The Bible is very clear that unconditional acceptance and love are to be our standard for living. To be operating any other way puts us in conflict with biblical truth. Being true to God's Word, then, means that we (and our students) are adjusting our lives to the truth that we are to out-love and out-accept the world.

2. Are students coming to faith in Christ?

We have functioned in youth ministry for too many years under the assumption that teenagers coming to faith in Christ are the product of our communication skills, evangelism programs, and outreach events. But students trusting in Christ are more often the result of relational bridges and relayed truth than they are preaching and programs. The issue is relational, not programmatic. Teenagers *not* coming to faith in Christ are a sign that unconditional acceptance and love are missing.

3. Are students' priorities changing in accordance with truth?

We cannot judge the heart of a teenager. We can, however, evaluate changes in a teen's priorities. Priorities do not change through sheer information consumption; they change as a result of life-on-life influence. They are caught more than they are taught. Unconditional acceptance paves the way to the kind of influence that can cause a major priority shift.

4. Are core students developing significant relationships with unbelievers?

The answer to this question requires little debate. Do our students have an agenda with their friendships? Are they investing and inviting? Are they withstanding Max Q for the sake of unbelieving friends? If not, their love quotient is definitely low.

5. Are core students excited about bringing their lost friends to youth group?

Our youth ministries reflect acceptance only to the degree that our core students are passionate about bringing their unbelieving friends to the environments we create. Remember the turtle. If our students aren't excited about bringing their friends, it's probably because they know their friends wouldn't feel accepted and would only stay in their shells.

6. Do guests feel welcome?

Many youth ministries are like a family that invites someone into their home and then ignores the guest once he or she gets there. If lost students do not feel welcome in our youth ministry environments, the issue is not the lights, the sound system, the song selection, or the facility. These are important things; but the real issue is acceptance—or, better stated, the lack thereof.

7. Are new students being easily assimilated?

This is not an organizational issue; it's a relational issue. If acceptance and love do not permeate our environments, then students will struggle to connect to the life of our ministry. Our front door may be huge, but that does us no good if our back door is wide open. Acceptance and love keep the back door closed so that students connect and stay.

8. Are students developing quality friendships with other students in our ministry?

Our youth environments should be places where teenagers in our communities can find great friends. In *The Seven*

Checkpoints, we asserted that friends determine the quality and direction of our lives. Shouldn't the students that a teenager meets in our ministries be people of the greatest quality—people who know how to point others in the direction of "the most excellent way"? If a teenager struggles to find quality friendships among our students, acceptance is obviously unplugged and out of order.

9. Are we identifying and developing leaders?

The biblical model for disciplism is one of multiplication, not addition. A ministry should be made up of circles (multiplication), not rows (addition). That means that to effectively disciple students, we must multiply, divide, and multiply again, over and over. And we must identify and develop new leaders in the process. The more we multiply, the more we have to divide, and the more leaders we need to effectively express love and acceptance.

10. Are our programs effective in achieving our mission?

It's so easy for us to commit ourselves to a certain program or event. But if that program or event has lost its effectiveness, for the sake of relationship, we have to be willing to make the hard call. Do we have the courage to chuck a program that is not helping us accomplish our mission? Keep in mind, people split churches over the kinds of stuff we may need to eliminate. Here's the question that must stay at the forefront: "Is this the most effective way to relationally connect with students?" The point is to stay committed to people, not programs.

A Lesson in Influence from Mickey Mouse

Recently Stuart's family spent several days on vacation at Disney World in Orlando, Florida. In the middle of all the fun, Stuart managed to learn an important lesson on influence from Mickey Mouse. Here's how he tells it:

> We loved everything about Disney World. Day after day we laughed and played until we were exhausted. All those roller coasters, movie characters, and theme rides can sure take it out of you!
>
> We decided to culminate our time with the Fantasmic show at the Disney-MGM Studios. We had heard rave reviews from friends about this awesome light show, but words fall short. You really have to experience it to believe it. Fantasmic takes place in an amphitheater with thousands of seats overlooking a large lake. A giant, manmade mountain in the center of the lake serves as the stage.
>
> The show begins just as darkness sets in. Bright lights pierce through the sky. A symphony of music reverberates through the air. Mickey speaks and dances at center stage. A forty-foot wall of water shoots up in front of the crowd and serves as a screen for video clips from Disney classics. Unbelievable!
>
> At one point the mountain splits open and becomes a huge fire-breathing dragon. Sweet little Mickey Mouse becomes Terminator Mickey ("I'll be bock") and kills the dragon. Disney characters come out in boats in full force. Fireworks burst and crackle in the night sky . . .

Did I mention the video clips of classic Disney movies on the forty-foot wall of water?

Fantasmic is Disney's way of pulling out all of the stops and saying, "Look how bad we are." It is Disney in all its glory. We sat spellbound for forty-five minutes.

After the show I was beside myself. I was like Tom Brokaw after the president's speech: I started recounting everything I had just seen and heard. I looked at my oldest daughter and, with great excitement and expectancy, asked her what her favorite part of the show was.

"Omaree," she answered.

Quickly I mentally reviewed all the Disney characters I could remember. "Omaree" did not compute. So I asked, "Honey, which movie was Omaree in?"

Omaree was not a Disney character. She was the little girl from Tuskegee, Alabama, who sat in front of my daughter at the amphitheater. The two girls had befriended each other before the show. They had talked and laughed about all the things they had seen and done at Disney World. And in a way that only children have mastered, an immediate connection had been made. They accepted one another completely. They were lifelong friends—in five minutes.

Omaree was my daughter's favorite part of the glory of Disney World.

May our students learn to be so unconditionally accepting of others that, in the glory of their lives in Christ, a relationship with a lost friend becomes their favorite part.

Pressure Points

1. "If friends determine the direction and quality of teenagers' lives, and if teenagers develop friendships according to who makes them feel accepted, then the people who make them feel accepted will eventually become their friends and will impact the direction and quality of their lives." How can you, as a youth leader, capitalize on this principle?

2. Discuss this statement with your leadership team: "Having the spiritual gift of evangelism doesn't free you from showing love to others. Love, as a fruit of the Spirit, supercedes the gifts of the Spirit."

3. What does the fact that Jesus didn't just fall to earth, say "uh-oh," and decide to die on the cross for humanity have to do with your students and unconditional acceptance?

4. How do you measure unconditional acceptance in your ministry? What tool or tools do you use to evaluate how well your students are doing in this area?

5. Would you say that your ministry to this point has been one of addition or multiplication? Explain.

I think the dilemma is whether
the believing students, the followers
of Jesus, are going to cloister
together and keep singing worship
songs over and over and enjoy their
faith and their walk with Christ
'til the end—or whether they're going
to let God's heart start beating inside
of their heart. If that happens,
it's going to break their heart and
propel them outside of their circles
and outside of their buildings.

LOUIE GIGLIO

PRINCIPLE 5

The Sustained-Influence Principle

Sustaining the Influence You've Gained

It's no secret that we live in a culture of immediate gratification and instantly met needs. These days we can, in a matter of minutes, drive through and order our lunch, pick up our dry cleaning, withdraw our money, and wash our car. We can drive through just about everything. We even have mortuaries that we can drive through to view a deceased loved one.

Then, of course, we have the miracle of modern surgery to make us thinner and more attractive overnight. My wife and I watched in amazement as a single guy on a reality TV show got calf implants to make his calf muscles bigger. Apparently he was in pursuit of an instant, perfect calf muscle. Working out was taking too long, so he decided to have implant surgery to obtain his objective *now*.

People will go to hefty extremes for the sake of immediate satisfaction and comfort! And none of us is immune to this dynamic. We may not be the plastic surgery types, but each of us has developed a certain level of impatience. If something begins to take longer than we expected it to, we can easily lose focus and motivation. I will be the first to confess that I have, on numerous occasions, quit on a check-out line that was not moving fast enough. More candidly, I have quit on relationships that did not materialize in the timing or way I expected.

It's as if we have a built-in clock inside us that sounds an alarm when things start to draw out too long. If that clock ever strikes midnight, we don't hesitate to move on to something or someone else.

This type of mindset is pervasive in our society. And it's an enemy of influence. For many of our students, the idea of immediate accomplishment carries over into the realm of influencing their peers for Christ. It certainly bleeds into our evangelism models and practices in youth ministry. We want teenagers to receive the free gift of salvation found through faith in Christ *now*. And if *now* is later, then we move on. After all, aren't there too many other teenagers who don't know about God, who need his love, and who may be more likely to bend to our methods of persuasion?

Don't get us wrong. Our students should have a passion to see their friends come to Christ. But the idea of immediate accomplishment as it relates to evangelism does not sit well with the example we have of Jesus in the Gospels. Jesus was never in a hurry. He never operated as if he were under a time crunch. Consider this parable he told to certain people of his day (the Pharisees) who had a mindset similar to our own:

> Suppose one of you had a hundred sheep and lost one. Wouldn't you leave the ninety-nine in the wilderness and go after the lost one until you found it? When found, you can be sure you would put it across your shoulders, rejoicing, and when you got home call in your friends and neighbors, saying, "Celebrate with me! I've found my lost sheep!" Count on it—there's more joy in heaven over one sinner's rescued life than over ninety-nine good people in no need of rescue.
>
> Or imagine a woman who has ten coins and loses one. Won't she light a lamp and scour the house, looking in every nook and cranny until she finds it? And when she finds it you can be sure she'll call her friends and neighbors: "Celebrate with me! I found my lost coin!" Count on it—that's the kind of party God's angels throw every time one lost soul turns to God. (Luke 15:4–10 *The Message Remix*)

Notice the shepherd didn't say, "Well, I have ninety-nine other sheep that need my attention and care. Losing one is no big deal." The woman didn't say, "Well, I have nine other coins. Losing one is no big deal." No, both the shepherd and the woman searched frantically until they found what they were looking for. They left the found to search for the lost. And they didn't find what they were looking for immediately. The unspoken implication here is that it took time for the sheep and the coin to be found. This shepherd and this woman were willing to invest whatever amount of time it took to find what they were looking for.

Our propensity in youth ministry is to not be so patient. The events we plan and the witnessing strategies we employ are predicated on a very high expectation of immediate return. Maybe we are unveiling a taboo secret here; but the truth is, some churches and church leaders have an irrational and almost humanistic expectation about "decisions made for Christ." Again, we're not saying that it's wrong to desire those decisions. But when it comes to lost teenage America, the majority of teenagers will require months if not years of sustained influence in order for God to unravel their past, address their present, and satisfy their questions to the point that his beauty becomes too overwhelming to resist.

For this reason it's vital that we develop students who reject the mindset of "if at first you don't succeed, find someone else." We must develop students whose influence is not so superficial that it fades like a summer tan. Our core students must be able to consistently influence their friends over time. Most of their peers will not immediately give their lives to Christ. For the majority, in fact, the process will be long and difficult. The leverage our students need in order to help their friends move from seekers to followers is riveted in sustained influence that stands the test of time.

The Power of Consistency

A hypothesis in the relatively unknown field of chaos theory says that a butterfly fluttering its wings in one part of the world can set in motion a chain of events that will lead to a hurricane in another part of the world. Which makes you wonder: Just how big is this butterfly? Are we talking a pterodactyl-like, Jurassic Park-sized butterfly? How come we don't hear about this butterfly on the Weather Channel? It sure would give a whole new meaning to the song "Butterfly Kisses."

It's hard for us to believe that the simple, repetitive movement of a butterfly's wings could end up causing hurricane-force winds. But seemingly impossible things like this are proven true all the time. For example, science has shown that a piece of cork, exerting consistent force over time against a wrecking ball hanging from a crane, will eventually move the wrecking ball. If enough time is allowed, the cork will eventually move the wrecking ball with enough force to actually destroy something.

This picture of consistency over time is a perfect illustration of the sustained influence we are suggesting. Our students are the butterfly wings. They're the cork. Their standards, priorities, accountability, and unconditional acceptance, lived out consistently over time, create the staging ground for sustained influence with their lost friends.

Don't Ever Change

Teenagers long for consistency in their lives. To them, consistency is like some weird form of human gravity: It holds everything down and keeps it all together. It helps them understand the world and their place in it. Things in their lives must hang together and make sense or they will be thrown for a loop. We see this played out in a dramatic way any time one of their peers dies suddenly or a tragedy falls into their world unexpectedly. Such inconsistencies create major dilemmas in their hearts and minds.

We will even go a step further: Teenagers *expect* consistency. When students wake up in the morning, they expect to find the floor under their feet, the roof above their heads, and a can of Coke in the refrigerator. And just as students expect this type of physical consistency, they also expect psychological and emotional consistency. If they had friends, families, and jobs yesterday, they expect to find those friends, families, and jobs in pretty much the same condition today.

If this were a perfect world (which it's not, thanks to Adam and Eve's stop at the fruit stand), everything in our students' lives *would* be consistent. But the world isn't perfect. Inconsistencies happen. Things change. Life says to our students:

Yes, there is a very good chance the floor will be under your feet when you wake up tomorrow. It is highly probable that the roof will be over your head. And if you didn't go on a caffeine binge the night before, you may very well find a soda in the fridge.

But Mom and Dad may divorce. Your best friend may move to another state. You may not make the team. You may lose your place at the head of your class. And—perish the thought—something awful may happen to someone close to you.

At some point all teenagers will have their own 9/11, surreal and unimaginable. Along the way, many smaller inconsistencies will surface between what they expect and what they actually get.

Their birthday comes around, and instead of the digital camera they were hoping for, they get a Snoopy electric toothbrush.

Their worst enemy compliments them on their outfit.

Their parents forget to attend the big game.

Mom and Dad decide that love is no longer worth fighting for.

Inconsistencies like these and others create a state of "dissonance" in teenagers. *Dissonance* is the technical term for the cognitive, emotional, physiological, and behavioral state that develops when things do not go the way we expect them to. A better term might be "emotional static." When we experience emotional static, we get a sense of mild confusion, a feeling of interruption: "What? What? What was that? I don't get it. Wait a minute!" We feel upset, anxious, a bit out of control. On a physiological level, our heart rate elevates, blood pressure goes up, and our hands get sweaty.

It's not a pleasant state! If Merck or Pfizer made a pill that gave people dissonance, no one would buy it. The only thing we want to do with dissonance is get rid of it. We want to get back to the state of consistency, back to the place where things make sense and that awful static isn't pounding in our heads.

Stopping the Static

Teenagers have devised a number of different tactics for getting rid of dissonance, all involving certain mental gymnastics:

Deny the Inconsistency

Just pretend it didn't happen. Ignore it. It's not there. Never was. Never will be. Next item.

Some students are better at denial than others. If you're not the type of person who lives in occasional denial, you may think this option sounds almost unbelievable—especially when you consider extreme circumstances, such as denying that Mom and Dad divorced or that a friend moved to a different continent. But amazingly, we have seen this option in action with teenagers in all kinds of situations, big and small.

Override the Dissonance

The goal here is to drown out the inconsistency with a ton of good thoughts and memories. Students can get a rough sense of just how much dissonance they are experiencing by the number of "good" thoughts they must come up with to override it. The more thinking required, the greater the dissonance.

Change Your Expectation

Let's go back to the example of the teenager who receives the Snoopy electric toothbrush as a birthday present. He or she might counter the obvious dissonance by reasoning, "There will be other birthdays. It's silly to get so fired up about one particular birthday. This one really isn't that special." The student changes the initial expectation, bringing it down to a level that is consistent with the lesser reality. Some people might call this "rationalizing."

Change Your Evaluation

Think again about the toothbrush. The student might say, "Wow, what a beautiful electric toothbrush! It must have cost a fortune. Think how long my dad had to shop around to find such a special gift!" Now, the teenager in this case is being serious. He or she is not just putting on a public face to cover up the disappointment. Rather, instead of responding with dissonant thoughts (*I can't believe I got this lousy toothbrush*), the student is actually changing his or her evaluation in order to reach the best, most consistent conclusion.

The key point is this: Teenagers feel driven to these kinds of mental gymnastics because dissonance is such an unpleasant state for them. They'll do just about anything to stop the mental static and restore consistency.

I Get It!

With all that said, you'll probably be surprised at this next statement:

One of the primary goals of a student of influence is to produce dissonance in lost teenagers.

Most lost teenagers have a relatively comfortable set of expectations about the world and how it works. Since changing their thinking would mess with their comfort level, they try to avoid change like the plague.

But change is exactly what has to happen if teenagers are ever going to come to faith in Christ. The job of our core students is to live their lives and interact with their peers in such a way as to create a sense of inconsistency—a feeling that something doesn't quite measure up—in their lost friends. Unfortunately, most of our students don't create enough emotional or spiritual static to be influential. They're unable to generate dissonance because their lives are too consistent with the lives of their lost friends.

Inconsistencies are a necessary factor in the process of influence. Conversely, they are also a big reason why teenagers hesitate to give their lives to Christ. For students to trust in Jesus, they will have to face many inconsistencies in their lives. Those inconsistencies will produce dissonance. If the inconsistencies are significant, and if our students don't stay consistently and closely involved, the static can become so overwhelming that it drowns out all thoughts of belief.

That's why it's imperative for our students to develop sustained influence in their friends' lives. They can't be flash in the pan. Most lost students will have to trek across a desert of inconsistencies to arrive at the oasis of belief. And they will need our students beside them to even begin to attempt such a journey.

Don't Look behind You

Dissonance has a tendency to follow teenagers. Students in middle school and high school always have issues. They always have someone who hasn't met their expectations. There is always tension. There are inconsistencies all around.

It's precisely this natural fact of teenage life that creates such an unbelievable platform for our students to be influential.

We need to encourage our students to love their friends unconditionally, regardless of the inconsistencies or differences that arise. Our students need to be so consistent, so trustworthy, so predictable (in a good way) that emotional static actually paves the way for them to gain leverage with their lost peers. They must be the consistency in the midst of the inconsistencies. That's the only way for them to gain the leverage of sustained influence.

The Ingredients of Sustained Influence

Influence is a double-edged sword. A person can use the principles of sustained influence to positively or negatively influence others. Obviously, our goal is to develop students who can influence their friends in a positive way to move toward faith in Christ. The ingredients of that kind of sustained influence are threefold:

Acceptance

Pardon the constant reference, but the fact that this first ingredient pops up so regularly in our discussions speaks volumes about its importance. The hallmark of Jesus' ministry was his willingness to accept the unacceptable—the outcasts, the sinners, the unlovable people. Acceptance was the staple of his sustained influence.

That's why it's so heartbreaking to us that many unbelieving teenagers feel unaccepted by the church. Christ didn't make people feel that way. As Christians we believe that certain things are right and certain things are wrong, and we have difficulty accepting people who are doing the wrong things. We think that accepting them means lowering our standards. But Jesus wasn't lowering his standards by accepting sinners. He wasn't condoning people's behaviors or lifestyles by loving them. He was simply doing just that: loving them. He loved them so much that he hated what sin was doing to them.

North Point Community Church is full of people who disagree theologically with us. It's full of people who are over their heads in lifestyles and habits that are contradictory to God's design. Our youth ministry is full of these kinds of teenagers. Yet they like us. They want to be around us. They appreciate and reciprocate the acceptance that we show to them. And as a result, we are able to continue to pave a path of influence in their lives and draw them nearer and nearer to faith in Christ.

The inability of the church-at-large to accept people who are different—whether in appearance, belief, or behavior—says more about our insecurities than it does our spirituality. And when we as youth leaders encourage our core students to ostracize teenagers who exhibit sinful lifestyles and habits, we are making a statement about our insecurities, not our spirituality. What's our purpose, after all? Lost students don't become more hungry and thirsty for God by having our students reject them. That thought process makes no sense whatsoever.

There are certain laws of acceptance that govern the degree of influence we have in the lives of others:

The Law of Sacrifice

Many years ago Shane Claiborne of the Philadelphia-based ministry The Simple Way arrived in Calcutta, India, to apprentice under Mother Teresa. When prayer time came, this humble nun removed her shoes, as was her practice. Claiborne found that he could not stop staring at her feet, because they were so grotesquely deformed. Afterwards, Claiborne asked one of the sisters what kind of illness had left Mother Teresa's feet so malformed. The sister answered him, "Mother Teresa's feet were not born like that. When people give shoes, she always waits to the very end and takes the shoes that no one else wants." Over time her feet had twisted and contorted to take the shape of ill-fitted footwear.[1]

Mother Teresa served those who needed God the most, even at the risk of her own comfort. And in that process she carved an incredible path of influence that is still circling the globe years after her death.

Mother Teresa exuded acceptance because she operated under the law of sacrifice. This law states that we are open to the influence of those who serve by making a sacrifice for something we consider important; we are closed to the influence of those who are unwilling to sacrifice when sacrifice is deemed necessary.

The emergence of a new respect for firemen and policemen after their heroic efforts on 9/11 illustrates this law. Heroes and heroines have influence in our culture; those who avoid sacrifice often do not. When Bill Clinton ran for president, Republicans tried to make a case against him on the basis of the law of sacrifice. They contended that since Clinton had eluded the draft in his younger years, he was not worthy of the office of Commander in Chief.

Our students need to understand that when they serve, they become models of acceptance and living examples of the heart of God to their peers. Serving may involve taking time to visit a friend in the hospital. It may mean canceling much-anticipated plans in order to give emotional support to a classmate who is going through a tragedy. It may be as simple as stopping to hold a door open for someone whose hands are full.

Acceptance means serving those who need God the most. Sacrificial service paves the way for sustained influence.

The Law of Empathy

Acceptance also means listening to those who need God the most. People don't behave a certain way without a reason. They don't think the way they do without a reason. The lost teenagers in our schools and communities act and think the way they do for a reason. If our students would learn to listen to their unbelieving peers, they would come to understand the "why" behind their friends' "what"—the reasons behind their friends' actions, habits, and lifestyles.

Ultimately, God's desire is to heal the "why." That's his focus. The "what" will take care of itself when the "why" is transformed.

Most teenagers, by their words and actions, are virtually shouting to us about the issues of their lives. Too often we're just not listening. I know that after reading the first two chapters of Marilyn Manson's autobiography, I suddenly understood the "why" behind his "what." Now I can honestly say that it would be no stretch for me to love him as Christ loves him, strange makeup and all. If only we would transfer that kind of understanding to the countless students who frequent the malls, stadiums, and schools in our communities! They all have a story. They all have a "why" behind their "what."

What we're talking about here is another law of acceptance: the law of empathy. It states that we are open to the influence of those who demonstrate an understanding of where we are and how we feel; we are closed to the influence of those who communicate insensitivity to our situation. A person may have the very insight or knowledge we need to transform our lives. But in most cases, unless the law of empathy is in operation, we won't receive it.

Empathy is powerful. It's why counselees often begin to develop feelings for their counselors. It is also one of the main reasons Jesus was so influential. Think about some of the things he said to people: "Come to me, all who are weary and heavy laden. . . . Blessed is the man. . . ." His teachings made clear that he knew what the people around him were facing and feeling. When most religious leaders were doing all the talking, Jesus listened—not only with his ears, but also with his eyes and heart. He was accepting and empathetic to people's needs, and it gained him leverage.

The Law of Beginnings

Our students cannot expect to gain sustained influence in the life of a friend by standing on the sidelines of his or her life.

Acceptance means becoming active in the lives of those who need God the most. Our students have to jump in and get connected—early on, if possible.

One student we know has done exactly that. Lauren is a strong Christian who has a close friendship with a girl who is not a believer. Whenever this friend is in trouble, she calls Lauren. Many nights Lauren has found her friend intoxicated and puking over the toilet, and she has stayed to take care of her. She has listened to her friend talk endlessly about boyfriend woes and lifestyle issues. Plenty of times Lauren has been ready to call the relationship quits and move on. But she can't. God won't let her. Her participation in her friend's life is building a superhighway of influence. And one day, in God's timing, the evidence of her influence will reap eternal benefits.

There is a sense in which timing is everything. A quick study of the world of gangs and cults tells us that people gravitate and stay connected to the people who love them first. This is the law of beginnings, and it is so powerful that it's almost irreversible. We are open to the influence of those who are first.

This law is why professional athletes stay true to their friends from "back in the day" and travel with entourages. It is why most of us can remember the names of those teachers who introduced us to a compelling topic, subject, or idea for the first time. It is also the reason why teenagers in the midst of transition are so vulnerable. They will all too easily get involved with the first person who comes along who offers them a sense of acceptance, whether that relationship is ultimately healthy or unhealthy for them.

Think of the law of beginnings this way: If you're building a new house and you've already poured the foundation, put up the frame, wired the electrical outlets, and put in the plumbing, it does no good for friends to show up and offer suggestions for a better floor plan. They may be right, but they are too late. Their influence is necessarily limited.

The same principle applies to lost teenagers. The degree of influence our core students have on their lost friends very much depends upon how soon they get involved in their friends' lives. The greatest potential for influence comes from being there first.

Competence

Another ingredient of sustained influence is competence. We are open to the influence of people we respect because of their competence in a particular arena; we are closed to the influence of those for whom we have lost respect (or never respected in the first place). We are open to the influence of those whose words are supported by their actions; we are closed to the influence of those whose actions contradict their words.

The influence of our students with certain friends hinges on their competency. Whatever our students do, they have to do their best. Our students must excel in the arena in which God has planted them. Paul put it this way: "Whatever you do, do your work heartily, as for the Lord rather than for men;

215

knowing that from the Lord you will receive the reward of the inheritance. It is the Lord Christ whom you serve" (Colossians 3:23–24 NASB).

Paul commands the people he is addressing (in this case, slaves and masters) to be the best they can be, whatever their role or position. The point is clear: Our work has eternal implications, even if it has no apparent eternal value. Some of our students may have plans to "move on" into full-time Christian service, which is a great vocational goal. But they must understand that their responsibility right now is to do the best they can in the environment in which God has placed them; namely, school. They are called to demonstrate their faithfulness to God right now—at school—by how they talk, how they act, how they show love and acceptance, and so on.

But behaving well is not enough. They have to perform well too, particularly in the areas in which God has gifted them to excel. Great character does not make up for poor performance. We try to help our students understand competence through this lens:

I will do my best at what I do best and give others an opportunity to excel at the rest.

Too many students are consumed by the lie that says they have to be great at everything: the best student in the classroom, the best athlete on the field, the best leader in the group. But no one person can be great at everything. It's impossible. Our students need to learn what their strengths and weaknesses are. When they work within their gift mix, they operate in their proverbial "zone." They become like Michael Vick scrambling in the open field. At school they have a zone they should work from with all their heart. With friends they have a zone they should be working from. It is when they are in this zone that their competence is best displayed and influence is gained.

And it's when they're in the zone that they honor God by their competence. Our students honor him whenever they recognize and make full use of the strength, resources, and gifts he has given them. They honor him by asking these questions continually throughout their lives: "How can I harness all that I am, all that I have, and all that I can do for the purposes of God? How can I apply my skill, reputation, network, or resources in a way that brings honor to God? How can I take my competence and leverage it for God's sake?"

These are the kinds of questions that can force teenagers outside the boundaries of church and organized religion. They are questions that, if fully embraced, could very well launch our students on a mission.

Gifts from God

To ask and answer these questions, however, students must be willing to recognize two things. The first is this: All the strength, influence, and resources we have are gifts from God.

We guarantee you that some students will resist this idea. They will argue that they were the ones who worked hard, studied hard, got up early, took advantage of opportunities. And they may well have done all of these things. But ultimately, the motivation, opportunities, and principles that

217

made their efforts possible were from the Lord.

Throughout Scripture we see that God gifted people and placed them in various positions for his purposes: Moses, Esther, Daniel, Deborah, Nehemiah, David. Each of these men and women were people of unquestioned competence and strength. Yet they knew the source of everything they had. David spoke for all of them when he prayed,

> Yours, O LORD, is the greatness and the power and the glory and the majesty and the splendor, for everything in heaven and earth is yours. Yours, O LORD, is the kingdom; you are exalted as head over all. Wealth and honor come from you; you are the ruler of all things. In your hands are strength and power to exalt and give strength to all. (1 Chronicles 29:11–12)

Our students need to understand that competence has been given to them by God and for God, to honor God. Their talents, skills—even their arena of influence—have not been given to them for their own sakes. They have been given to them for his sake.

An Eternal Direction

Some students may continue to resist this thought until they recognize a second point: Jesus committed all of his competence, strength, and power to their good.

In our culture and in Scripture, hands are a symbol of strength, power, and competence. Jesus used his hands to feed the hungry, heal the sick, hold little children, wash dirty feet, and touch lepers and corpses. Through his hands he displayed his unparalleled competence as a leader, teacher, and savior. But at the end of Jesus' life on earth, his hands were drawn up into helpless, grotesque claws as nails were pounded into his wrists, right through the carpal tunnel that houses the finger-controlling tendons. When he rose from the dead, the only leftovers from the trauma of crucifixion were the nail scars in his hands:

A reminder of how he spent his life.

A reminder of where he focused his energy.

A reminder that he did not come to be served but to serve and give his life.

Jesus channeled his competence, power, and strength in our direction, for our good, and he asks us to do likewise: to channel the competence, power, and strength he has given us towards others. How can our students say no? How can they continue to harness their competence for their sakes alone and, at the same time, claim to be followers of the one whose strength was poured out for them?

You know what's so ironic? All that we do for ourselves with our competence will pass away with us—the things we build, the stuff we gather, the pressure we bring to bear. We will never make a mark by spending and consuming, only giving. When we die, the only thing we will leave behind are the investments we have made on behalf of others.

We don't forget the people who, in their lifetimes, put their competence to work for our benefit. Ultimately, the people who leave their mark on the world are those who apply their power and strength on behalf of something bigger than themselves.

Do you want to develop students who build an enduring

kingdom? Then make sure they build that kingdom outside the walls of their own little world and all of its small, petty wants and needs. Do you want to develop students who apply their strength to something that lasts? Then make sure they work towards something bigger than the enrichment of their own lives, because what they build for themselves won't last. They must focus their competence in the direction of eternity.

Authenticity

The final component of sustained influence is authenticity, which we define as consistency between what we say and what we do—between what we claim to be and who we really are. Jesus was so influential because he was exactly who he claimed to be. Those who knew him best were the ones who trusted him most. What a great litmus test for authenticity!

We resist the influence of people who are not what they claim to be. Inconsistency between what is said and what is done cripples influence. Very few of us are willing to follow someone who is a blatant contradiction in terms. We're not open to their influence because they're not real; we can't trust them.

Jesus challenged his followers:

You are the light of the world. A city set on a hill cannot be hidden; nor does anyone light a lamp and put it under a basket, but on the lampstand, and it gives light to all who are in the house. Let your light shine before men *in such a way* that they may see your good works, and glorify your Father who is in heaven. (Matthew 5:14–16 NASB)

Notice the emphasis we have added: "*in such a way.*" The implication is that our students' lives should be lived with such authenticity that others take notice and begin to model that lifestyle. In *The Message*, Eugene Peterson paraphrases verse 16 so beautifully when he says, "By opening up to others, you'll prompt people to open up with God, this generous Father in heaven."

Teenagers are watching. They want to find duplicity in our students. They figure that finding a contradiction let's them off the hook. Our students earn their influence by walking their talk. A lack of authenticity on their part damages any potential they have for influence.

Isn't This Underhanded?

When we've shared the principle of sustaining influence with teenagers, we've heard one objection repeatedly from Christians and non-Christians alike: "Should relationships really have an agenda? I mean, for students to try to achieve sustained influence in the lives of their friends just so they can share the gospel with them—doesn't that reek of insincerity? It almost seems underhanded! It makes friendship little more than a ploy."

We answer that question with this question: Was Jesus being underhanded when he did all that he did in order to accomplish his agenda? Was he being insincere when he was busy loving people and convincing them he was the Messiah?

The answer to this second question depends on what his agenda was. The answer to the first question depends upon whether or not our students have that same agenda.

If there is some kind of "gotcha" attached to the agenda our students have, then absolutely, what they're doing is underhanded and wrong. If our students (and we as youth leaders) are somehow profiting off of someone coming to faith in Christ, then our agenda is insincere and we have moved into dangerous waters. We should not be paying a commission (monetary or any other kind) for every teenager who comes to faith in Christ. There is no quota system. Our students should not be collecting points to go to Disney World based on the influence they gain in a peer's life. If our agenda of sustained influence has any fraction of selfish gain as a part of its makeup, we have to step back and rethink what it is we say we're about.

The reason we teach about leveraging influence over time is that we believe Christ offers a cure for life's three biggest problems: sin, sorrow, and death. God has entrusted us, his followers, with the cure. We would be the most self-centered and selfish of all people if we kept that cure to ourselves. Sharing this cure with the people around us must be the driving motivation of our hearts and lives. It must be the driving motivation of our students' hearts and lives.

A Legacy of Sustained Influence

One of Mother Teresa's first projects in Calcutta, India, was to turn a former hostel into a hospice where the poor, who often died alone in the streets, could spend their last hours in comfort and cleanliness. From the start, the Catholic sisters faced alienation and neighborhood hostility, much of it emanating from the Hindu temple next door. The poor and dying have bad karma, according to Hindu belief, and the Hindu priests felt that caring for such people only interrupted their destined and ordained end.

The priests tried to get city authorities to relocate the newly named Nirmal Hriday, or "Home for the Dying." But then one of the priests was found to be in the advanced stages of tuberculosis. Denied a bed in a city hospital—beds were limited in number and reserved for those who could be cured—this representative of the enemies of the Catholic order ended up in a corner of Nirmal Hriday, tended by Mother Teresa herself. When the priest died, she delivered his body to the temple for Hindu rites. News of this charity filtered out into the city, and Calcutta started its long love affair with Mother Teresa and the humble sisters.[2]

Mother Teresa's story is a perfect illustration of what consistency over time can achieve. Her unconditional acceptance of even her enemies—people who wanted to destroy her—gained her great leverage in Calcutta and eventually around the world. Her competence in hospice care was unrivaled. And she was everything and more than she claimed she was. She became a living, tangible example of the heart of God to millions upon millions of people. Now, Mother Teresa didn't have the opportunity to share Christ personally with every one of those millions of people. And certainly, many of the people she touched never accepted Christ as Savior and Lord. But her influence and leverage was unmistakable.

If the world chooses not to believe our message, let it be said of our students that they have been the most accepting, competent, and authentic group of teenagers anyone has ever seen. Such qualities may not get immediate results; but our students can rest assured that they will lead to the kind of sustained influence that can eventually change the world.

Pressure Points

1. How does the modern cultural desire for immediate satisfaction affect your efforts to influence your students?

2. What is the danger of students having a mindset of, "If at first you don't succeed, find someone else"?

3. Do you think teenagers expect consistency? Why, and in what ways?

4. "If our students would learn to listen to their unbelieving peers, they would come to understand the 'why' behind their friends' 'what.'" Why is this statement important? Do your students struggle with listening for the "why" behind the "what"?

5. As an individual and as a ministry team, evaluate your influence with students as it relates to this statement: "We resist the influence of people who are not what they claim to be."

The spiritual man habitually
makes eternity judgments
instead of time judgments. . . .
Such a man would rather be useful
than famous and would rather
serve than be served.

A. W. Tozer

9

The Leverage Principle

Using Your Influence Wisely

Our problem with student evangelism is not the gospel. Our problem is that we are developing a generation of Christian students that has zero leverage with its peers. The gospel has not lost its power; rather, our students have lost the ability to influence their friends. They have not built relational bridges strong enough to bear the weight of truth. Consequently, scores of teenagers in your community and mine have never had the truth of Christ transferred to their hearts. They have never experienced the kind of defining moment that would alter the course of their eternity.

For far too long, we in youth ministry have assumed we know how to gain leverage with unbelieving teenagers. But contrary to popular belief, a cool environment does not equal leverage. The fact that students show up at an event doesn't mean that we now have leverage in their lives. Just because lost students answer their front doors when we knock doesn't mean we have gained enough leverage to speak truth to them.

Without a real, viable relational bridge in place, our students' efforts to relay truth to their unbelieving friends will be difficult at best. At worst, lost students will be so turned off that they will never lend a Christian a listening ear again. But when our students focus on building relational bridges, the job gets a whole lot easier. We can almost guarantee that as our students gain influence this way, opportunities will open up for them to talk about their faith, ask hard questions, and challenge their lost friends' belief systems.

Of course, leverage gained and never used is no leverage at all. Our students must come to a point of *trusting the trust* they have established with their unbelieving friends. That point, then, becomes a defining moment for our students *and* their friends. What our students and their unbelieving friends do in that moment will mark them. It will even determine the direction of the rest of their lives.

How our students exert and extend their leverage with their friends is critical. We can't afford to assume. We can't risk failure with a one-size-fits-all mentality. Our students must be wise. This is hazardous work we are preparing them for. Jesus compared it to a sheep running through a pack of wolves. Our students must be "as cunning as a snake, inoffensive as a dove" (Matthew 10:16 *The Message*

Remix). They must handle the leverage they have earned with care and use it appropriately.

The Mind of a Teenager

Which takes us back to some of the sociological aspects of influence that we discussed in chapter 3. To briefly recap, we said that there are two relatively distinct modes of thinking that teenagers employ. The first, the "systematic" mode, refers to critical thinking. The thought processes of systematic thinkers are active, creative, and alert. These are the students who find holes in a Christian student's testimony and ask questions that cause believing teenagers to doubt their own salvation!

The second mode of thinking is "heuristic." Students in this mode are not thinking carefully; they're skimming along the surface of ideas. They are aware of what a Christian peer is saying to them, but they are not thinking conscientiously enough to catch any flaws, errors, or inconsistencies in the statement.

This current generation of students is extremely flexible in its thinking ability. It can move back and forth between the two modes, often depending upon situational and personality factors. This means that no single factor (except for the Holy Spirit) is a guaranteed path to leading an unbelieving student to trust in Christ. Depending upon the individual teenager's mode of thinking, some things will work and others won't. Different types of spiritual leverage will have different effects on different kinds of thinkers.

This dynamic makes identifying a particular student's mode of thinking very important. When a teenager is in the systematic mode, certain things will be influential: facts, evidence, examples, reasoning, logic—what we call "apologetics." When a student is in the heuristic mode, however, apologetics will be ineffective. Facts, evidence, and reasoning require too much cognitive effort. Easier-to-process information will be better suited to heuristic thinkers—things like attractiveness, friendliness, or excellence. We call such things "clues."

Ultimately, influence achieved through the systematic mode is more consistent over time, more resistant to change, and more predictive of behavior than influence achieved through the heuristic mode. When teenagers are thinking systematically, their decisions are more likely to stick, mainly because they have thought about them more carefully, fully, and deeply. Heuristically-based decisions are likely to be more short-lived, simply because the students didn't really think about them that much.

And therein lies the challenge: We want unbelieving students to change, and we want the change to last. That means we want students to use systematic thinking. But generally speaking, most teenagers think heuristically most of the time. They think just enough to meet the minimum demands of the situation.

What can be done to make heuristic-thinking students begin to think more systematically? Two factors are key.

The first is *relevance*. When unbelieving teenagers believe that a certain body of information is personally important to them, they will be much more likely to think about it systematically; if the information seems to hold little relevance to them, they will stay in the heuristic mode. This means that our core students must demonstrate how a relationship with Christ can be meaningful and relevant to the lives of their unbelieving peers. They must live such radical lives of faith that their lost friends are motivated to—oh my goodness!—think.

The second factor is *comprehension*. Many of our efforts to influence fail simply because lost teens cannot comprehend the appeal. When our students present a gospel that is complex, dense, and obscure, their friends have to work too hard to understand it, and they drop back into the heuristic mode. Our students must encourage systematic thinking by making sure they share the deep truths of God's Word in a way that is easy for lost teenagers to remember, understand, and apply.

My Apologies

Once students are thinking systematically, they need apologetics. But which set of facts, arguments, and evidence will be most effective in reaching them? That depends upon the questions a particular teenager has. "Relative apologetics" may seem like a contradiction in terms, but it expresses an important concept.

Consider teenagers and smoking. In the past, persuasion sources (parents, teachers, the federal government) have tried to prevent teenage smoking by offering health-based evidence: "Smoking causes cancer." A statement on every pack of cigarettes gives facts and the surgeon general's opinion on the health-related perils of smoking. Yet teens continue to smoke. Why? The health argument doesn't grab them. It doesn't seem relevant. Teenagers embrace the myth of their own immortality; they believe they will live forever—maybe even to forty. Threats of cancer and early death are empty to them.

Newer approaches are using different arguments, however, and they are getting better results. The new arguments are based on social factors: "You will smell bad if you smoke." "No one wants to kiss somebody with cigarette breath." The importance to teenagers of peer acceptance and approval makes these arguments much more relevant and powerful. It is not that the facts and evidence about the perils of smoking have changed. It's that the public-service announcers have chosen to attack the problem from a more relevant angle.

Here's the point: For our students to effectively use apologetics, they must understand what and how their lost friends are thinking. They must tailor their apologetics for relevance.

One of the most difficult things about Christianity is that, on the surface, it seems like a lot of wishful thinking—a hope-filled dream that when we die, everything will work out. This is why, when our students try to talk to their friends about their faith, the general response is, "That's good for you, but here is what I believe . . ." The tendency is to think that Christianity is just one of many good world religions.

But it's not just one more good religion. It is distinct in a number of ways. For one thing, most world religions believe you have to be good and do good things to get to heaven; Christianity says you can be bad and still get to heaven. (Makes you wonder why more people don't come to Christ.)

The most significant distinctive about Christianity, however, is one that often gets overlooked in outreach to teenagers, mainly because we try so hard to be practical. We teach students to say, "Before I came to Christ, I was that way . . . but now, since Christ came into my life and changed me, I'm this way." That's great information to share, as long as the primary distinctive is not ignored or forgotten.

What the Foundation Is Not

That primary distinctive goes to the very foundation of our faith. Contrary to popular belief, the foundation of our faith is not the teachings of Jesus Christ. The teachings of Jesus are extremely important; but the fact is, all world religions are based on *somebody's* teachings. Christianity was not established on what Jesus taught.

The foundation of Christianity is not a philosophy of life. Most world religions subscribe to a certain way of life—certain lifestyles, habits, and disciplines. People must follow that way of life if they want to be considered devout disciples worthy of eternal reward. Christianity is not based on a way of life. Yes, the Bible teaches us how to live, but that's not what Christianity is built on.

The foundation of Christianity is not a country. Teenagers are not Christians because they were born in America. That's like saying that being born in the trunk of your car makes you a spare tire. Other world religions seem to draw inspiration from geography. Hinduism has India. Judaism has Israel. But Christianity is not based upon where you were born.

The foundation of our faith is not even faith itself. Our faith is not based on our ability to believe. We don't just *believe*. Besides, what kind of foundation would that be—

especially for students? They change what they believe about things practically every day.

What the Foundation Is

So what, then, is the foundation—the primary distinction—of our faith? *An event.* Christianity is based on one event that took place one morning over two thousand years ago.

Not on the teachings of Christ. (There were lots of teachers in that day.)

Not on the crucifixion of Christ. (Many of those teachers were killed or died.)

Not even on the fact that it works. (That's just an added bonus.)

Our faith is based on the resurrection of Jesus Christ.

All other world religions and movements started with a prophet, leader, or group of people who died, either through martyrdom or natural means. Their disciples said, "Keep the dream alive!" and began spreading the teachings of their prophet or teacher or group. Every world religion other than Christianity started this way.

You know what Jesus' followers did when Christ was crucified? They were so discouraged that they went back to fishing. They were so afraid that they huddled in a room, scared to death. Keep the dream alive? They were thinking, "Keep *me* alive!"

If Jesus had simply been a teacher of good things, then when he died his friends could have said, "Keep the dream alive!" and spread his teachings. But Jesus went too far. He said things like:

- "When you see me, you see God."

- "God and I are one."

- "The only way to God is through me."

- "I'm going to die and rise from the dead in three days."

Jesus so closely connected himself to God that when he died, the dream died. If he was God, his followers reasoned, then would God allow himself to be killed? In the minds of the disciples, the death of Jesus meant the end of the cause.

But here we are, over two thousand years later, not because of what Jesus said, not because of miracles, not even because he died on the cross. We are here because people saw a dead man walking. Jesus Christ rose from the dead and appeared to over five hundred people in the forty days after his resurrection and before his ascent.

In that time period, thousands of Jewish people in Jerusalem, the heart of Judaism, abandoned hundreds of years of heritage and embraced Christianity. Why? Because people were walking through the streets of the city saying, "I saw him!" Cowards who ran when Jesus was arrested, who denied knowing him when confronted, who wouldn't even watch him die, were claiming that he was alive and preaching Good News!

Peter and John faced their own deaths not because of something they believed. They faced death because of what they saw and heard. Peter was crucified upside down. John rotted away in exile. James, the half brother of Jesus, was martyred. Because of what they believed? No. Because of what they *saw*.

That's the reason Paul exclaims, "And if Christ has not been raised [from the dead], our preaching is useless and so is your faith" (1 Corinthians 15:14). *The Message Remix* paraphrases it this way:

> If there's no resurrection, there's no living Christ. And face it—if there's no resurrection for Christ, everything we've told you is smoke and mirrors, and everything you've staked your life on is smoke and mirrors. Not only that, but we would be guilty of telling a string of barefaced lies about God, all these affidavits we passed on to you verifying that God raised up Christ—sheer fabrications, if there's no resurrection. (1 Corinthians 15:12–15)

How much more leverage could we want? Jesus rose from the dead to verify his identity and validate our faith. And if a guy can rise from the dead, I don't care what he taught—I'm with him! He could tell me to wear a grass skirt and puka beads and run up and down the beach singing the theme from *Sponge Bob*, and I am doing it. You conquer death, and I am following you. Why? I don't want to die! I'm afraid of death—not so much of *being* dead, but *getting* dead.

And so are countless numbers of teenagers who are asking our students hard questions. The resurrection of Jesus is the best distinctive we have to share with teenagers who are in a systematic thinking mode.

Get a Clue

But what if a teenager won't budge out of the heuristic mode? Is it still possible to find a point of leverage with a heuristic thinker? Absolutely. That's what clues are for.

Clues can be very powerful. If you don't believe us, watch the beer commercials on TV. Attractive young women in skimpy clothes are the dominant images in these ads. No reasonable person would claim that these young women are arguments for drinking beer (unless you believe that the girls come with the six-pack). The images certainly don't turn audiences into systematic thinkers about comparative beer quality. No, the ads simply offer a clue. People (usually men) watch the beer commercials and see the attractive girls. They like what they see in a way that requires little thinking on their part. And they simply associate that good feeling with beer.

Influence without thought. It works!

Christian students can exercise leverage with their heuristic-thinking friends in a similar way. They can live such magnificent lives of beauty, joy, and peace that the Christian life becomes too attractive for their friends to ignore. They can use the word pictures of Scripture to describe how great our God is.

Consider Isaiah 40, for example. The prophet asks, "Who has scooped up the ocean in his two hands, or measured the sky between his thumb and little finger? Who has put all the earth's dirt in one of his baskets, weighed each mountain and hill?" (verse 12 *The Message Remix*). What a picture! Our Creator is so huge that he can pick up the oceans of the world in the hollow of his hand. He carries the dust of the earth around in a beach pail. That's a big God!

Isaiah continues,

Who could ever have told GOD what to do or taught him his business? What expert would he have gone to for advice, what school would he attend to learn justice? What god do you suppose might have taught him what he knows, showed him how things work? (verses 13–14)

In other words, no one has ever told God what to do. No one has told him how to be God. He never went to a psychiatrist or counselor for advice. He never attended Harvard Business School. He doesn't need anyone to teach him anything.

Interestingly, Isaiah communicates most of this information about God in question form. He gives heuristic thinkers a picture and then challenges them to think about it.

Watch him sweep up the islands like so much dust off the floor! There aren't enough trees in Lebanon nor enough animals in those vast forests to furnish adequate fuel and offerings for his worship. All the nations add up to simply nothing before him—less than nothing is more like it. A minus. (verses 15–17)

The more I read these verses, the smaller and smaller I become!

In verse 18 Isaiah confronts his listeners with a choice: "So who even comes close to being like God? To whom or what can you compare him?"

Our students can lead their heuristic-thinking friends to a similar moment of reckoning. Whether by words or implication, when they present God in all his glory, they ask, "Isn't our God huge, wonderful, amazing, beautiful? Who can compare—that jock who thinks he owns the football field? The guy who thinks he's God's gift to the opposite sex? The gorgeous girl who just won homecoming queen? That computer geek who's so smart, he could break into Fort Knox with his laptop?"

What a clue! Scripture, Creation, life and all of its lessons—they are chock full of clues that our students can point to. If students aren't sure what mode of thinking a friend is using, we tell them to remember this catchy phrase:

What to do? Get a clue.

It's always wise to paint a beautiful picture of God's greatness and might. It's always right to paint a beautiful picture of the compassion and wisdom of Jesus. When our students lift Jesus up, he will draw people to himself. That's his promise in John 12:32. Even systematic thinkers can't help but be moved.

The Implications

Five important implications unfold from the recognition that different students use different modes of thinking—and are therefore more open to some forms of leverage than to others:

1. Our students must learn to read their unbelieving friends.

Students can figure out the thinking mode of an unbelieving friend by observing that friend's nonverbal behavior. Generally speaking, if a teenager's behavior indicates attentiveness, alertness, and thoughtfulness, he or she is probably in the systematic mode. If a teenager's behavior demonstrates distraction, boredom, or laziness, he or she is probably in the heuristic mode. As our students become more adept at reading their friends, they will be able to use their leverage more effectively.

2. Our students must learn the art of asking pertinent questions.

Students must learn how to ask good questions and then judge the quality of their friend's responses. Do the answers sound thoughtful and reasonable? That indicates the systematic mode. Does the friend give answers that are off the wall, or does he or she continually say, "Could you repeat the question?" That indicates the heuristic mode.

3. Our students must learn to match the right influence tool with the right thinking mode.

You don't need an umbrella on a sunny day. And students who are thinking heuristically will not heed apologetics. Our students have to identify their friend's mode of thinking correctly and then provide whatever is appropriate: apologetics or clues.

This is probably the biggest mistake students make in their attempts to use their spiritual leverage. Our core students can become extremely frustrated if they develop great arguments or clues and then see them fail because they weren't the right tool at the right time.

4. Our students must learn how to use clues more often.

As we have said, when teenagers think systematically about apologetic evidence, the influence our students bring to bear on them is longer lasting, more resistant to change, and more likely to motivate a change in behavior. We want that. That's why we spend so much time training our students in the presentation of apologetics. But the fact remains that most teenagers think in the heuristic mode most of the time. That means we must teach our students how to use clues and encourage them to use clues more often.

5. Our students must learn to develop arguments from the point of view of their lost friends.

During the mid-1980s, Burger King spent millions of dollars on a major advertising campaign designed to challenge McDonald's for leadership in the competitive fast-food market. The campaign was built around a character named Herb—a balding, thin fellow who wore glasses, black pants that were too short, and white socks. Herb was supposed to be a whimsical sort of "Every Man" that all of us could identify with.

It didn't work. No one identified with Herb. In fact, there were a lot of Herb jokes in those days. The ad campaign totally backfired; and instead of running for a year, it was killed in a month. Somehow Burger King had terribly misread the market and produced messages that no one found compelling or influential (or even enjoyable).

Our students can do the same thing if they are not careful. They can offer arguments that *they* find compelling and powerful, assuming that their lost friends will have the same opinion. Bad assumption.

The best way for our students to develop leverage is to carefully observe their friends. Really listen to them. Ask them about the music they like and the movies they watch. Pay attention to the clothes they wear and the language they use. Students who tune in to their friends this way will develop an intuitive sense about what will and will not be effective.

Building the Bridge

To have the most leverage possible, our students need to identify more than their friends' mode of thinking; they need to determine where their friends are in the journey of faith. Some teenagers have never even heard of Jesus. Some have a degree of knowledge, and they are interested in learning more about how Jesus can change their lives. Other teenagers are very close to making a decision to place their faith in Christ. Still others are actually walking with him.

Disciplism, in a nutshell, involves building a bridge of relationship with lost students and then using the appropriate leverage to move those students across the bridge one step at a time. The type of leverage that is used and the degree to which it is used depends upon where teenagers are in this five-step process:

Step One: "Huh?"

At this step students don't even know that Jesus exists. They've never heard of him. Never seen a Bible. They have no clue what this gospel thing is all about. They live in a state of benign ignorance that says, "What you don't know won't hurt you." Teenagers on Step One know nothing about why they were created, or the relationship between hell and their sin nature, or why they need grace and mercy and forgiveness. And because they don't know, they don't care.

Also at this step are all those teenagers who know about Jesus and the cross but see absolutely no reason to respond. To them, having a relationship with Jesus is irrelevant. What he did doesn't matter, because they don't think it relates to who they are and what they are about.

Paul speaks of the state of "Huh?" in his letter to the church in Rome. He asks, "But how can people call for help if they don't know who to trust? And how can they know who to trust if they haven't heard of the One who can be trusted? And how can they hear if nobody tells them? And how is anyone going to tell them, unless someone is sent to do it?" (Romans 10:14–15 *The Message Remix*).

Most of our students' unbelieving friends are at this step. The simple truths of Scripture are foreign to them. The Bible is not a viable entity. Our students must be sensitive to this fact. The worst mistake they can make is to assume that a friend knows more than he or she knows.

Step Two: "Oh!"

At this step teenagers have seen the difference Jesus has made in the life of a friend. They have heard the gospel, realize there may be something to it, and are seeking answers. Students at this step want to go to church or youth group. They ask to borrow a Bible. They start talking with their friends about God stuff. They ask questions that most of our Christian students have never even thought of.

At North Point, students often start attending our discipleship environment at this step—before they make a decision to trust Christ. They like having their questions answered in a small group of Christian teenagers who care about them. It's a safe place, and they feel the freedom to be vulnerable and transparent. Does the presence of unbelievers disrupt the discipleship process? Not at all. In our experience core students (especially those who have grown up in church) benefit from having seekers in their group asking difficult questions.

Asking and answering questions is as much a part of disciplism as any other facet we consider foundational to the process. As Solomon exhorted his son,

> If you accept my words and store up my commands within you, turning your ear to wisdom and applying your heart to understanding, and if you call out for insight and cry aloud for understanding, and if you look for it as for silver and search for it as for hidden treasure, then you will understand the fear of the LORD and find the knowledge of God. (Proverbs 2:1–5)

The implication is that seeking answers leads to understanding.

Besides, discipleship doesn't mean that every student must be reading John Piper or Jerry Bridges, keeping a journal, and praying three times a day while facing their denomination's national headquarters. That's a paradigm that we in youth ministry have perpetuated for too long. It borders on being pharisaical. Disciplism is not a destination. It's a process. Spiritual depth in our students isn't measured by the information they know but by the transformation they show.

Step Three: "What?"

Teenagers at this step are weighing their options. They are carefully evaluating what they will lose and gain by trusting in Christ. This step takes time. It's tedious. It may seem to go on forever. But it's absolutely necessary. Students who take this step are the ones who will "stick."

Consider these words of Jesus to the masses who followed him: "Suppose one of you wants to build a tower. Will he not first sit down and estimate the cost to see if he has enough money to complete it?"(Luke 14:28). Jesus goes on to explain how foolish it would be for someone to start something he or she had no intention or ability to finish. He continues: "Or suppose a king is about to go to war against another king. Will he not first sit down and consider whether he is able with ten thousand men to oppose the one coming against him with twenty thousand?" (verse 31). Jesus' point is that those who want to follow him need to carefully consider the consequences and ramifications of doing so.

Two things are critically important at this step: relational connections and a patient ministry culture. We can't rush a teenager to judgment. We can't use "Stupid Church Tricks" to try to persuade a teenager to trust Christ. Rather, we must train our students to be patient, hang in there relationally, and exert leverage only according to the pace at which their friend is crossing the bridge.

Step Four: "OK!"

Students take this step when they are willing and ready to trust Christ with their lives. This is the moment our students have worked so hard for. It deserves to be celebrated. It warrants a party. Heaven throws one. So should we!

In the last chapter, we looked at a passage of Scripture that challenges us to seek that which is lost. That same passage tells us what to do when the lost item is found:

And when he finds it [the lost sheep], he joyfully puts it on his shoulders and goes home. Then he calls his friends and neighbors together and says, "Rejoice with me; I have found my lost sheep." I tell you that in the same way there will be more rejoicing in heaven over one sinner who repents than over ninety-nine righteous persons who do not need to repent. . . .

And when she finds it [the lost coin], she calls her friends and neighbors together and says, "Rejoice with me; I have found my lost coin." In the same way, I tell you, there is rejoicing in the presence of the angels of God over one sinner who repents. (Luke 15:5–10)

If we're not careful, we can lead students to believe that Step Four is the finish line—that if they will just trust, they're set. Trusting in Christ as Lord and Savior definitely determines their eternal destination. But it does not guarantee them the eternal life the New Testament speaks of that refers to their quality of life in Christ on earth.

Countless numbers of people make New Year's resolutions to start a new diet, and they hang tough for a few weeks. But by mid-February, they're back to their old eating habits. Similarly, tons of students make decisions to trust Christ, yet they struggle to actually follow him when the rubber meets the road. This fact only emphasizes the critical importance of disciplism. Our students' influence must not end when their friends reach this trust step.

There is still one more step to go.

Step Five: "Let's Go!"

Step Five is the process of transformation. At this step teenagers begin to live the Christ-life without having to plan it out or think about it so much. Their new, eternal life becomes a normal part of their daily routine, like brushing their teeth every night.

How long does it take for the Christ-life to become a visible manifestation of the invisible miracle that has taken place in a student's life? That depends. Renewal is a process—one that involves identifying the old lies that once served as the pattern for life and replacing them with Truth. Paul puts it this way:

> Since, then, we do not have the excuse of ignorance, everything—and I do mean everything—connected with that old way of life has to go. It's rotten through and through. Get rid of it! And then take on an entirely new way of life—a God-fashioned life, a life renewed from the inside and working itself into your conduct as God accurately reproduces his character in you. (Ephesians 4:22–24 *The Message Remix*)

If the new way of life were as simple as learning to use a DVD player, our students would get it down almost instantaneously. But the transformation we are talking about is much more significant and deep-seated than becoming adept with a DVD player. Many students come into the Christ-life with serious baggage. Many have horrible, hard-to-break habits. Others are deeply involved in extreme lifestyles.

Transformation takes time. Following Christ goes on forever.

One Step at a Time

The bridge-building business is not an easy one to gauge. Anything that has to do with relationships is hard to measure. We don't know how long a particular student's bridge will have to be. We don't know how many weeks, months, or years it will take a particular teenager to get from Step One to Step Five. The only thing we know is that whatever the length of the journey, it must be traveled one step at a time. For this reason our bridge-building students—our students of influence—must remember three things:

1. Tailor the influence tool to the step.

It would be foolish for our students to approach an unbelieving friend on the "Huh?" step (ignorance) the same way they'd approach someone on the "What?" step (considering). But by knowing what step a friend is on, they can tailor their influence with an eye to a very focused goal: moving that friend to the next step. If a friend is at the "Oh!" step (learning), for example, then our students' leverage goal is to move that person to the "What?" step (considering).

2. Build the bridge one step at a time.

Our students can't expect their lost friends to move from Step One (ignorance) to Step Five (following Christ) in one giant leap. Rather, they need to focus on building the bridge one plank at a time, exerting just the right amount of leverage to move a friend through each of the steps in order.

3. Don't settle for a half-built bridge.

Building a complete bridge can take a very long time, especially if an unbelieving friend has started at Step One or Step Two. Our task as youth leaders is to encourage our students not to grow weary or impatient or quit in the process. We need to develop students of influence who are committed to building a relational bridge one step at a time, at the pace that is best suited to their friend's journey of faith.

Leverage in Action

Kelsey's freshman year of college promised to be a major adjustment, to say the least. She had decided to go to school away from home, which meant living on a campus and in a town where she didn't know a soul. Because of a snafu in room assignments, she was initially housed in an athletic dorm room with nothing more than a cot and a hanging rack. Needless to say, when she received the news that she would be moved into a permanent room situation, she was ecstatic. She didn't care who her roommate was. She just wanted her own drawer space!

Kelsey's new roommate was a Hindu girl named Pratima. Pratima's family was originally from India but moved to the United States so their daughter could receive a better education.

The girls' first night together was full of conversation. Kelsey was intrigued but a bit uneasy with the chants Pratima had written on the bathroom mirror, the Hindu figurines she had placed around the room, and the potent smell of curry that permeated the air. They discussed religion and, to

Kelsey's surprise, Pratima knew as much about Jesus as Kelsey did. In fact, Pratima was very knowledgeable about Christianity—she just wasn't interested in following it. She was devoutly Hindu.

Over the next few weeks, Kelsey made several unsuccessful attempts to persuade Pratima to accept her way of thinking. Kelsey had witnessed to people before; she had even led people to Christ before. But she couldn't budge Pratima. *Why is she so challenging?* Kelsey wondered.

One reason: They were roommates, and Pratima was watching Kelsey day in and day out. Each evening when Kelsey had her quiet time, for example, Pratima took note. One night Kelsey came in very late and decided that at that moment, sleep was more appealing than spending time with God. As she slithered into her bed, Pratima (who Kelsey had assumed was sound asleep) spoke up from her bed on the other side of the room. "You didn't spend time with your God today," she said matter-of-factly, her face turned to the wall.

Kelsey immediately jerked up in bed and turned on her bedside lamp. "You're right, I didn't. Thank you," she said, opening her Bible.

At that moment Kelsey realized something important: The point of her relationship with Pratima was not to persuade her with clever arguments to choose Christianity. It was to live the Christ-life in front of her in a way that would cause her to crave it.

Kelsey had never been faced with such a monumental challenge: to live a life of godly standards, right priorities, accountability, and unconditional acceptance before another person over a sustained period of time.

To be in the midst of maximum dynamic pressure and not only survive but thrive.

She spent an entire semester gaining leverage with Pratima and then learning how to exert that leverage effectively. She learned how to ask pertinent questions that forced Pratima to defend and question her own belief system. Sometimes simply pointing to the beauty of God was influence enough. At other times she and Pratima engaged in serious dialogue about the evidence and proof of Christ's resurrection.

Much time passed before Pratima began going to a worship gathering of college students that Kelsey attended. Eventually Pratima started attending a Bible study with Kelsey, where she asked many hard-hitting questions. By the time their living arrangement ended, Pratima was open to the idea of accepting Christ.

Your students and mine will have a Pratima in their lives. Maybe not a person of a different religion or culture. But a classmate. A neighbor. A teammate who needs to know Jesus. How will they leverage their lives for the name and fame of God?

Are You Ready for Liftoff?

The bottom line is that our students have a choice: Will they simply hang in there through their teenage years, hoping to somehow survive the pressures of modern teenage culture with a modicum of faith intact? Or will they allow God to work in them and teach them to become students of real influence in their world?

251

As youth leaders and parents, we also have a choice: Will we leave the spiritual development of our students to whim and chance, hoping that the intervention of God will make up for our lack of vision and influence? Or will we choose to invest the life-changing truths of the principles in this book into the hearts and lives of our students?

Shhhhh. Can you hear it? We can. It's the awful whistling sound of maximum dynamic pressure bearing down on you, your home, your ministry, your students. And it's getting louder every day.

Our role as youth ministers is difficult yet so significant. We must create ministry environments that simulate and breed influence. We must develop students who can withstand Max Q and not break apart under pressure. Students who can be light in dark places. Students who will not waver from their faith while passionately pursuing relationships with their peers. Students who can earn influence and the privilege to be followed.

Essentially, you and I are launch directors. Our job is to prepare students and then send them off into exciting, purposeful, influential lives—lives focused on knowing God and making him known to a world that desperately needs him.

Are you ready? Then let's pick up the count:

Five . . . four . . . three . . . two . . . one . . .[1]

Pressure Points

1. Do you tend to communicate with students from a heuristic perspective or a systematic one? How would you rate your effectiveness?

2. How can you adjust your programming to communicate to both heuristic and systematic thinkers?

3. Discuss this statement by A. W. Tozer with your leadership team: "The spiritual man habitually makes eternity judgments instead of time judgments. . . . Such a man would rather be useful than famous and would rather serve than be served." What do "eternity judgments" have to do with leverage?

4. If disciplism is not a destination but a process, what does this say about how our students appropriate leverage in their lost friends' lives?

5. Thinking back over the life of Jesus, how would you say he appropriated the leverage he obtained?

The key to successful leadership today
is influence, not authority.

KENNETH BLANCHARD

Epilogue

The joke is told that at the beginning of the 2003 military conflict in Iraq, Secretary of State Colin Powell put a haughty Iraqi reporter in his place.

"Isn't it true that only 13 percent of young Americans can locate Iraq on a map?" the reporter asked.

"That may be true," Powell answered. "You're probably right. But unfortunately for you, all 13 percent are marines."

God is not concerned with the *quantity* of students who desire to be influential. His concern is with the *quality* of students. He is not looking for influential students he can make faithful. He is looking for faithful students he can make influential.

When the young Americans who know their geography are marines, "how many" is irrelevant. And when the students we develop and send into the hurricane-force of maximum dynamic pressure are students of godly standards, right priorities, maintained accountability, unconditional acceptance, and sustained influence, "how many" is irrelevant.

The lives of countless numbers of hurting, petrified, and confused teenagers are breaking apart under the pressure of Max Q.

Someone has to have the courage to rescue them.

Will it be you?

Will it be your students?

Notes

INTRODUCTION

Epigraph. Jim Rayburn III, *Dance, Children, Dance* (Wheaton, Ill.: Tyndale House Publishers, 1984), 158.

CHAPTER 1: GRANTING PERMISSION

Epigraph. John Eldredge, *Wild at Heart* (Nashville: Thomas Nelson Publishing, 2001), 149.

1. From an interview with Josh McDowell at the May 2003 GrowUp Conference at North Point Community Church. The session was titled "Be Relevant."

2. *First Knight*, Columbia Pictures, 1995. Written by Lorne Cameron, David Hoselton, and William Nicholson. Directed by Jerry Zucker.

CHAPTER 2: KNOWING WHAT TO EXPECT

Epigraph. Erwin Raphael McManus, *An Unstoppable Force*, (Loveland, Colo.: Group Publishing, 2001).

1. From copyrighted resource material by Reggie Joiner, "Be Relevant," http://www.252Basics.org/, http://www.GrowUpon line.com/, (accessed 2003).

CHAPTER 3: UNDERSTANDING INFLUENCE

1. Jeff Cannon and Lt. Cdr. Jon Cannon, *Leadership Lessons of the Navy Seals* (New York: McGraw-Hill, 2003), 31.

2. Joiner, "Be Relevant."

3 Dr. Steve Booth-Butterfield, "Dual Process Models: from the online *Persuasion Primer,* 1995–2004, http://www.as.wvu.edu/~sbb/comm221/chapters/dual.htm.

4. Ibid.

PART TWO: THE PRINCIPLES

1. This is one of those urban legends that has circulated for years in various forms across the Internet. Some versions say the American scientists were from the Federal Aviation Administration; other versions say they were from the Air Force. In some versions, the British engineers are not British at all but from France or even America. Whatever the truth is, the point is still the same!

CHAPTER 4: THE STANDARDS PRINCIPLE

1. Mike Krzyzewski, *Leading from the Heart* (New York: Warner Books, 2000), 10.

2. Ibid.

3. Ibid.

4. Rudolph W. Giuliani, *Leadership* (New York: Talk Miramax Books, 2002), xiv.

5. Andy Stanley and Stuart Hall, *The Seven Checkpoints for Youth Leaders* (West Monroe, La.: Howard Publishing Company, 2001), 101.

CHAPTER 5: THE PRIORITIES PRINCIPLE

Epigraph. John Eldredge, *Waking the Dead* (Nashville: Thomas Nelson Publishing, 2003), 211.

1. Chris Tomlin, "Wonderful Maker," *Not to Us* (Brentwood, Tenn.: Sparrow/EMD, 2002).

2. Erwin Raphael McManus, *Seizing Your Divine Moment* (Nashville: Thomas Nelson Publishing, 2002), 65.

CHAPTER 6: THE ACCOUNTABILITY PRINCIPLE

1. Gregory Lumberg, "When Love Comes to Town," *CCM,* January 2001.

2. Krzyzewski, *Leading from the Heart,* 11.

CHAPTER 7: THE UNCONDITIONAL-ACCEPTANCE PRINCIPLE

Epigraph. G. K. Chesterton, *Orthodoxy* (San Francisco: Ignatius Press, 1908), 55.

CHAPTER 8: THE SUSTAINED-INFLUENCE PRINCIPLE

Epigraph. Janet Chismar, "Louie Giglio: Shaping a New Generation through OneDay03," http://www.crosswalk.com/fun/music/1198424.html.

1. Trinity Church Web site, "Don't Lose Your Footing," http://www.trinitytoledo.org/pdf/upload/SermoneEaster3B.pdf.

2. Subir Bhaumik and Meenakshi Ganguly, "Seeker of Souls," *Time*, September 15, 1997.

Chapter 9: The Leverage Principle

1. Expression and ideas in this chaper taken from the online *Persuasion Primer* by Steve Booth-Butterfield, West Virginia University, are used with permission from the author © 1991–2004 Steve Booth-Butterfield.

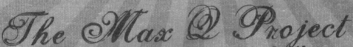